ΩMEGA TO ALPHA

MAXIMIZE YOUR POTENTIAL AND UNLEASH YOUR BEST SELF

DEJAN GARALEJIC

Storyline Publishing

Copyright © 2024 by Dejan Garalejic

All rights reserved. This book or any portion thereof may not be reproduced or used in any manner whatsoever without the express written permission of the publisher, except for the use of brief quotations in a book review.

ISBN (Paperback): 978-1-0689669-0-3
ISBN (eBook): 978-1-0689669-1-0

Cover design & Interior formatting by Aaxel Author Group

www.aaxelauthorgroup.com

This book is presented solely for educational purposes and entertainment purposes. The author is not offering it as professional services advice. While best efforts have been used in preparing this book, the author makes no representations or warranties of any kind and assumes no liabilities of any kind with respect to the accuracy and completeness of the contents and specifically disclaim any implied warranties of fitness of use for a particular purpose. The author shall not be held liable or responsible to any person or entity with respect to any loss or incidental or consequential damages caused, or alleged to have been caused, directly or indirectly, by the information contained herein. Individuals should seek the services of a competent professional.

I would like to dedicate this book to you, the reader.

At the end of the day, you are the most important person and the reason I decided to share my experience and knowledge.

Without you, this book would be useless.

Without your decision to do something with your life and better yourself, all this would be pointless.

So YES, I dedicate this to all of you who have found the strength to admit to yourself that you need to change your life.

That right there is the first and most important step towards a new and better future.

I wish you all the best on your journey to better yourself and if this is your first step, may there be endless more to follow.

Always keep a goal in front of you that will guide you and use the wind in your back to help you get there.

PROLOGUE

The world as we know it today, that we live in at this very moment, is rapidly evolving. This is the case now more than ever before.

Unfortunately, it seems more like a **devolving** process to me.

I observe and study people and their behaviour globally, and I can't help but fear for the future of our kind.

We've separated ourselves so much from our primal selves in this modern age that we've lost touch with the **real humans** we are all meant to be.

It seems we are doing everything in our power to silence that voice of the wild we all have inside us and, with a lot of help from the internet and social media, have managed to distance ourselves so much from our ancestors that it's become alarming.

Global awareness, through the power of the media and internet, has shifted toward forgetting the true values of humankind.

Strength, integrity, ambition, honesty, chivalry, honor, and bravery are frowned upon.

Strength is perceived as dangerous, ambition as selfishness, and integrity and confidence as narcissism.

Values that got us this far through the ages, such as sacrifice, hard labor, endurance, perseverance, courage, and fellowship, are now considered wrong, masculine, unfair, and undesirable.

All those true values are stigmatized to cater to the majority of the population, who have very little to offer in those areas. By making those traits undesirable, they are more easily rejected by modern society, helping those who lack the above-mentioned values feel better about themselves. Thus, fake "equality" is achieved.

New, emerging generations are progressively growing weaker in all aspects of life. This regression is evident in all areas of our existence. It's a physical, psychological, intellectual, and moral descent all at once, and it's spiraling out of control.

We have an army of self-doubting, weak, and undecided young people without a moral compass. Everyone feels entitled to everything they want, but no one wants to take any responsibility for their actions. People get hurt by words, need a "safe space" to deal with everyday problems, and have lost the ability to handle normal, in-person, social interactions. Everything revolves around text messages, e-mails, and various social media chat forums.

What worries me greatly is that, in nature, when a species becomes flawed, weak, and vulnerable, it soon becomes extinct.

The hard laws of nature don't tolerate the weak and undecided. That is how it's intended. Survival of the fittest.

So, if we follow that chain of thought, what can we expect to happen to humankind as a whole as we become more weak and defenseless?

Don't allow yourself to fall into that trap. Now, more than ever, Humanity needs strong, real individuals.

It needs LEADERS. There are enough FOLLOWERS. Don't settle for a life as one.

PROLOGUE

Transform yourself into an Alpha Lion and take what is yours. You will not only help yourself in the process but also inspire others to follow your example.

Be the change you wish to see in the world.
—Mahatma Gandhi

You will notice that I use many quotes throughout this book.

Many great people, as they forged a path through history, left a legacy behind, and we would do well to familiarize ourselves with those. Brilliant minds have come up with some essential facts, ones we should learn, take to heart, and live by.

All those great people, famous and anonymous alike, became aware of these and many other wise things and world truths. Their quotes still inspire us and help us find those verities within ourselves! Many of you felt inspired after reading one of these at some time or another. Maybe one day, if you become courageous enough to share those thoughts with the world around you, people will quote you too.

Among many others, I like to quote the great Chinese Taoist philosopher Lao Tzu.

The reason behind that lies partially in the fact that he is my favorite philosopher, and our views align most of the time.

The fact is, everything I teach here, he already talked about at length!

The quotes I include will show that much bigger minds became aware of these facts long before our time, but somehow, we've managed to forget them!

You will learn how my teaching revolves around these wise words.

Drawing parallels to and emphasizing old philosophies was **not** my intention when I started this project, but as I went along, pouring my thoughts into the written material, I became aware of this phenomenon.

My philosophy differs from Taoism in one very important area, however!

Where Lao Tzu suggests no action be taken and that all good things come to those who wait, I strongly believe in initiative and action! Maybe the time that has elapsed between then and now, or the extent to which our way of life has changed on a global scale, should be taken into account. In today's world, time has become the most valuable thing one possesses, and we can't afford to just sit around waiting for good things to fall into our laps.

I urge you, in fact, to take the steps necessary to achieve your goals in the shortest time. I don't know whether Lao Tzu would have taught differently in this day and age. I assume he would have changed his philosophy to match the changes in the world around us, but I stand by my belief!

Though I like and quote Tzu, I strongly feel that Russell Bishop's quote better reflects the base of my teaching and will help you to better understand what I want you to learn.

So, let this be the FIRST LESSON I teach you:

The universe rewards action, not thought!
—Russell Bishop

CHAPTER 1

INTRO

First things first!
If you purchased this book hoping it was another take on the Greek alphabet, you couldn't be more wrong!

Will you get a lesson in Greek? Not likely!

But was your money wasted if that was the case?

Definitely *not* if you finish the book!

Instead of learning Greek, you will MOST DEFINITELY get a valuable lesson to take with you and pass on to those you care about!

Keep reading, and you may find yourself in a mess you never expected to be in! You may experience revelations and a weird, heightened sense of self-awareness! It might trigger the need to better yourself. You might experience a sudden boost of confidence, a rush of new life goals, and mixed feelings about the world you live in and your place within it!

You will recognize the boredom of your present self and your life and become ready and eager to change in no time!

So, without further delay, let me explain what this book IS all about!

It's not about Greek, grammar, or language, though it will urge you to become as skilled and educated in those fields as possible!

It's not about history, though it will teach you things that have come to pass, as well as things that will change your understanding of your history, and with that, alter your future and that of many others you come into contact with!

It will teach you a thing or two about nature and laws; you'll learn more about the world, but the whole purpose of this book is to teach you about yourself. To reveal your hidden powers and strength, how to reach for them and make them work for you. It will help you prepare for anything life brings your way and guide you toward the right path when faced with many possibilities, all through self-respect, knowledge of your abilities, and newfound confidence!

It will give you the tools necessary to achieve greatness.

I want to be clear here.

When I say GREATNESS, I mean that you will become the best version of yourself and thus achieve your ultimate level of self-awareness and worth.

Does that interest you?

Of course, it does!

Who doesn't want to be more successful in all aspects of life? Who, today, doesn't need a little confidence boost, a little more faith in their abilities? Who in their right mind would rather not become a better version of themself?

In the pages that follow, I will give you the implements to achieve all that and more.

I will teach you (notice how I didn't say, "try to teach you") how to use those instruments and master the art of growing spiritually, intellectually, and physically!

I will also provide you with the information necessary to understand the world around you. Most importantly, I will help you find the endless possibilities hidden inside you. By reading this book, you will learn to unlock your potential, spread your wings, and become free. To distance yourself from the boundaries and limits others have set for you and

INTRO

discern how to sum it all up and use it to your advantage against the negativity, pessimism, and doubts we are surrounded by!

When you finish this book, you **will** become a New You!

A better, stronger, more confident machine capable of crushing its enemies and any obstacles in its path!

You will unlock your full potential and become successful in everything you set out to do!

The knowledge contained in this book will also improve your social and business life, help you reach your educational potential, bring you closer to the people who matter in your life, and rid you of those who negatively influence you. Those who are weighing you down as you struggle to swim upstream at this very moment!

You will set aside your fears and doubts.

You will meet this New You, the one you've hesitated to admit existed. But deep inside, you always knew your present life was just a shadow of what you were meant to be!

You will walk through your life tall and proud, speaking loudly and clearly while looking others straight in the eye from this point forward.

You will be heard and understood, and people will follow your lead as you set examples for others!

Give a man a fish and you feed him for a day.
Teach him how to fish and you feed him for a lifetime.

—Lao Tzu

But before you learn how to run, you must learn to walk. And even before that, you must bring yourself down to crawl.

To start that process, you must be born first. Therefore, let us start from the beginning and explore how you can take these necessary steps, with a little guidance...

Let's start with a simple little lesson first!

***Nature*…**so simple in its rules, so predictable in some ways, and yet so mysterious and hard to understand in others. Nature is full of amazing wonders.

We are fascinated by things we don't fully understand, things that still exert mystical power over our minds.

We like to think and write about these wonders, even capturing them in photos and videos. It all seems fascinating and magical… Rainbows, oceans, great falls, the Aurora Borealis, the Grand Canyon, the universe, and other things that let our imagination wander into realms of the unknown, untouched, and unexplored…

But I'm not here to talk about those things, no matter how fascinating they may be.

I'm going to talk about other, **Real-life** things, things that can help us survive in this hard-to-get-a-grip-on world that surrounds us. In this day and age, we can admire those beautiful things once we get home, take our game face off, hang our clothes, and treat ourselves to a hot bath and a glass of wine, savoring that little free time to ourselves and trying to make the most of it.

Now, before you take another soak in the tub, stop and ask yourself: "When was the last time I stopped to smell the roses?!"

MY POINT EXACTLY!

Now, ask yourself, **why is that?**

You know the truth; it is right there. Hidden between that old job that downgraded you recently. That cut down your already embarrassing income. And the new, part-time, just-as-dead-end job you finally accepted just to pay the bills! Right there in the middle of your hectic day, as your landlord asks for rent, as people on the street honk and yell while stuck in rush-hour traffic while battling their own demons. It's right next to you in that cubicle, where you spend your day crouched, hoping to get by unnoticed. You hear it in your headphone set, where the barking voices coming through it only add to your mounting stress. It's tied to the job that makes you hate yourself, your life, and everyone around you!

INTRO

It's in bed with your girlfriend and best friend while you're out flipping burgers until late at night to buy her an engagement ring in, what, fifteen to twenty years?!

YES! You know what I'm talking about. Seems like the whole world is against you. It's right there, sitting on your stiff shoulders, weighing you down, making it hard to breathe! And believe me, you are **not** alone in this...

But let us go back for a second...*WAAAAAY* back... Before us humans roamed this planet, destroying it in the process of our evolution...

So...*Nature!*

And its creatures.

It was supposed to be easy, you know?! Animals have simple rules. And they live and die by them without question!

ALPHA is the leader... The **OMEGAS** in the pack follow. Very simple and effective.

The Alpha is a specimen superior in strength and appearance, genetically predisposed toward dominance, and biologically engineered to have leadership abilities! It's easy with animals. Nature made sure of that!

Sex doesn't determine **ALPHA** status. Leaders come in male and female forms alike! Usually, in the animal world, the leader of a whole pack is male, with the Alpha female by his side. The Alpha's only concern is the other alphas, who eventually **will** step forward to challenge Him/Her. He knows it; he is ready for it. That's normal and nature's way of ensuring that the strongest and fittest always lead the pack! Alphas are good at recognizing each other, which, between two males, typically results in a battle to the death or close to it. Between opposite sexes, it creates attraction! Alphas are known for claiming multiple mates and, in some cases, all the females in the pack or herd!

So, to sum it up, Alphas are *FEW* because nature intended it that way. So, who are those other poor souls, you ask? The ones waiting in the back while Alphas feed, dreaming of a mate but never getting their turn, walking around with their tail between their legs and ears pulled back, showing respect to the pack leader? The ones you can draw parallels with but won't admit it to me or yourself just yet? Well, those are, ladies and gentlemen, the ones this book is **really** intended for...

THE OMEGA!

Now, if you stop reading here, having decided that this is not about you and is a waste of time, you fall into one of two categories. You are either an Alpha already, in which case you need not read this book, or you are an Imaginary Alpha (more on this topic later), and you should BY ALL MEANS read on. So, be honest with yourself. Re-evaluate your life and goals, what you've achieved, and where you want to be years from now.

Reflect **HARD** on your past.

Remember every time you regretted not taking action when you should.

The opportunities missed because of your fear of failure.

Potential partners you wanted to chat up but never did out of fear of rejection, and so you let some other person with piercing eyes, a straight posture, and superior confidence take advantage of your hesitation right in front of your nose. Even as that potential partner gave you clear signs of their desire to be seduced.

Remember all those times you possessed the knowledge to earn better grades in school and felt injustice after the teacher gave you a "B" or "C," yet never stood up for yourself?

Now do you begin to see? Nature intended this cycle for all animals, and it was proven perfect...

But somewhere along the lines, one of those miracles happened, and HUMANS were born into this world...

A Human! Creatures with highly developed brains. Humans learned to think, communicate, and solve problems beyond the level of any other animal on the planet. Later on, as it turned out, this species grew more capable of creating problems than solving them, but that is a discussion for a different book. I believe even Mother Nature herself was

INTRO

caught off guard by what She created! Unpredictable, moody, and curious, Humans soon became a threat to their environment and all other creatures alike! But most importantly, it became its own worst enemy.

We started to evolve…

For centuries, we changed, grew physically, and gained greater intelligence as we harnessed and flexed the gray matter that had developed so much more in us than others with which we've shared this world.

And we put it to good use, developing educational programs in which people could learn and excel academically, inventing, building, creating, and more, thus separating ourselves from all other earthly creatures to the point that we started to feel God-like.

But in all that power, arrogance, and ignorance, we forgot one thing.

We all came from the same place. No matter how much we've evolved or accomplished, no matter what **WE** like to believe, we are still bound to nature and its laws.

Despite all our triumphs, somewhere along the way, our course declined. Progress came to a halt.

And started to deteriorate.

I'm not talking about technology, science, or world development. I'm talking about progress as an individual. Our Human progress.

It seems that modern-era man has become too dependent on the technology we invented. Too much of that primal instinct for survival has been lost to the convenient lifestyle of the modern world. We rely on the laws we invent and blindly follow the instructions and restrictions in place to control the population and its behavior. Social, moral, and other standards and norms, invented and implemented by a few, to tame us and further distance modern man from its primal ancestor, are in effect.

The need to *FIT IN* based on our society's standards is greatly exaggerated through (social) media and the internet. People blindly follow current trends and copy the behavior of the majority out of the desperate need to be accepted socially by others who also follow the same patterns.

We've forgotten what and who we need to be and instead, let others judge our worth through modern society's prism.

Having said all this, let me really begin this journey by focusing on what really matters.

Lets talk about you. Who you realistically are, and who you're striving to become.

Maybe you're not even sure where to start, and most definitely where you want to end, but fear not. That's why I'm here, in your corner, to coach and guide you through this.

CHAPTER 2

DEFINITION

Your own positive future begins at this moment. All you have is right now. Every goal is possible from here.

—Lao Tzu

Face it: Our modern world, just like our ancient worlds, both known and unknown to us, functions in harmony with nature's laws. It's less obvious, hidden between layers of modern inventions, the fast pace of life, electronic gadgets, traffic, education, and science, but it is there, and it's inevitable. Just like that wolf pack, out in the wild, we live in an Alpha-driven society.

Those with strong skills excel in the world. Top world leaders, CEOs, billionaire businessmen, investors, motivational gurus, and many others who gain positions of power in today's world are Alphas who, at some point, recognized an opportunity and were the fastest and strongest to capitalize on it.

Now, the thing with humans is that Alpha status has become more than just a matter of brute strength and other physical capabilities! With animals, such traits are all that matter. Simple rules for simple creatures living in simple communities.

The strong and capable hunt, fight, and celebrate while the weak and cowardly stay back, cheer for those doing the work, and feast on the leftovers.

With humans, it's **VERY** different. The Alpha isn't always the physically strongest, fastest, or most capable specimen. When it comes to people, many factors determine that status.

There's more than one way to become powerful.
—Dejan Garalejic

This contrast is the result of that gray matter we carry around between our ears.

If you think about it, you'll realize that this is almost always true. Even for creatures dipped into the genetic pool longer and more generously than most, Mother Nature worked out a balance. That's why, when it comes to strength, muscularity, and other physical capabilities, nature compensated on the other end and granted such specimens less active gray cells to work with...

On the other side of the spectrum, the majority of academically strong, intelligent people—often referred to as nerds—lack in the physical department.

We could of course point out some extreme cases that bend the rules a bit, but as a general rule, nature likes to keep things at an equilibrium, without blessing certain specimens with all the advantages and instead giving a little here while cutting short there. In rare cases, there's a glitch in the system, and the Ultimate Alpha is born, but that's a rarity, and we won't be discussing such an unusual occurrence here.

I want you now to think about those animals for a minute. They are either the Alpha or the Omega, and they are okay with that. They spend their lives living as nature intended.

DEFINITION

They obey all the laws; they live and die by those rules. They don't know any differently or feel the need to change things for the better. In other words, they play with the cards they were dealt.

In my opinion, that is the main difference between us and all other species.

They see generation after generation going with the flow, and quite frankly, they lack the higher intelligence required to realize they could possibly change the course of their lives.

While animals accept nature's order and adjust to their environment as needed to survive, we humans gravitate toward bettering our current status and adjusting our environment to suit us better.

We have that advantage; we can think and decide for ourselves. We can bend if not beat some of nature's laws. There are so many examples of humans optimizing nature to suit our needs instead of the other way around.

We can tame rivers, create energy from natural sources.

We can stop nature's rage to a certain degree.

We can predict the weather somewhat and protect ourselves from natural disasters.

So, if we can make nature work for us to this extent, why haven't we managed to change our genetic predispositions?

Because, believe it or not, we have the capability to do just that!

For so many, this is nearly impossible to believe. Think about it. Realize which type you are! Do you need more physical strength, more endurance, a higher education? What is holding you back in life?

If you do not change direction, you may end up where you are heading.

—Lao Tzu

I'm not writing this book because I want to help you win a fist fight, look good shirtless on the beach, or be able to answer the next million-dollar question on a game show.

I want you to realize that we all have the potential to be Alphas. We have the resources available in this day and age. We hear stories of people curing themselves of an illness using nothing but sheer willpower and running when doctors gave up all hope they'd ever walk again.

People do unbelievable things every day. Graduating from a university at age fifty; competing and winning bodybuilding contests, along with fitness and strong man shows, even later in life and after so much time spent being unfit; or building business empires, starting with nothing but an idea and incredible willpower.

Little miracles happen all around us daily and are the result of people realizing their true potential and rising to the challenge, believing in what they can do and not quitting when times get tough! We all have an **ALPHA** inside us, but not everyone has the ability to unlock it. Some learn with time. Sometimes it takes an event so powerful that it shakes your very core and changes your course in life. Most times it never happens. But you should be aware that it's within you and up to you to find and unleash!

Again, none of this is meant to help you score with that hot person at the bar next door to your workplace or beat somebody at chess or in a wrestling match.

Make no mistake, however, that it *WILL* change your life! Believe me. Being Alpha is about control over yourself first, then others, and finally, your life!

It's about being a leader, not a follower!

By unlocking the Alpha within you, so much will transform. Others will look up to you; all eyes will turn your way when you walk into a crowded room. Just as in a Western movie, when the gunslinger walks into a bar and everything goes silent, with all eyes on him while a tumbleweed silently rolling across the still sands outside.

Yeah. Just like that!

DEFINITION

Well, *THAT'S* the reaction you'll garner everywhere you go!

I know... You think it's impossible. That you could never make such a dramatic change happen.

Which brings us to the first step in creating the Alpha personality! You need to **believe** you can do it.

As Henry Ford once said: "Whether you think you can or you think you can't, you're right!"

That's SO true! The only limits we have are the ones we set for ourselves. If we fear failure so much that we shelter ourselves from every risk, if we *never* attempt to reach *beyond* our limits, we will never grasp what our limits truly are!

None of this can happen on its own. You must want to change not just wish for it. You must make that decision, cut the cord that connects you to your old ways, let go, and be reborn into a new, better you! This means starting from scratch, from ground zero, with your old glass completely empty, ready for a new you, the **ALPHA YOU**, to be poured in right to the top and beyond! You must bury your old self; it will only hold you back *every* time you do something out of the ordinary, something daring and unorthodox, something only an Alpha would! Old You will try to resurface, will try to sabotage your success, be that little voice telling you it can't be done and ultimately, cause your failure!

So, before anything else, you must first let go of what you've been all this time: the **OMEGA!**

Unconditional, 100 percent free of that old self, the weak, scared you, all wrapped in a layer of excuses. Just KILL and bury it once and for all! Unless you think you can do that, can take that first step, there's no point reading on! Take your time and work on it if you have to before turning the page. It can't be done overnight; it's a process, but you can do it.

How? You have to want it...bad!

So bad you can taste it!

You have to be tired of being pushed around, of working jobs you hate, of coming home to an empty place... You need to break free, stand up straight, stick your chest out, square your shoulders, grab life by the horns, and realize *YOU CAN!*

Realize, this is what you want to do. What you are destined for! If you truly wish to leave a mark after you're gone, to make your life matter, if not for yourself then for generations to come, you have to stop surviving this life and start living it! Because you're worth it! Everyone is! And always remember:

---

*In the end, though, everybody dies,
but not everybody LIVES!*

—Mark Lawrence

CHAPTER 3

THE VOICE

You know that voice inside of your head, the one we sometimes call common sense, which tells us to *NOT* do certain things like take shortcuts, choose the easier way, take the road more traveled?

Do you realize who that is?

It's *YOU!*

You are the one questioning every move, doubting your reasoning, and procrastinating until your inner Alpha gets tired of it all and takes control.

You subconsciously put your Alpha-self to sleep and avoid doing things you know you should!

Be aware of that voice—it is your biggest enemy! Bigger even than all the naysayers, fear, and negativity you might encounter on the way!

It is so dangerous because it's often hidden from our conscious mind, buried deep inside layers of previous life experiences and memories! It is often disguised as a friend, as the voice of reason, as the sober side of you, and it's hard not to listen to it!

I'm not telling you to ignore it! I'm telling you to get rid of it...for good!

Yes, you heard me! Be done with it!

It's a plague, a virus, and it will slow you down. It will make you doubt yourself, your capabilities, and your decisions! And the biggest shock about this disease?

Are you ready?

It's NOT EVEN REAL!

You heard me right! It's self-generated! Artificially created and planted in your subconscious mind!

Think about it.

I'm not talking about alien abductions here or a secret government project.

I'm talking about everything this society teaches us. Laws, rules, etiquette, everything that bends our spine, makes us crouch and crawl. Everything keeping that Lion locked in a cage is working hard in conjunction with an ally and enemy of yours...

THE OMEGA in you!

Omegas and society together created that voice, made it seem like the voice of your conscience, and it will sabotage your every attempt at greatness! It will be your hidden menace, your downfall if you don't acknowledge and deal with it before starting your journey!

Repeat in your head: **"It is NOT real!** It is a product made to poison and kill every advanced idea and thought!"

Designed to pull you back and oppose, to make taking risks almost impossible, this product is the culmination of years of data-gathering, psychological tricks meant to pick your brain and harness your anxieties, exploiting everything that scares you most! This product is insidious, and it's been carefully put together by your worst enemies to impede your progress! Worst of all, it's incredibly effective.

That is why I'm emphasizing here, as the first step, that you must kill that old self, shed your doubts and fears like a snake does its old skin, drop the burden of modern society norms and boundaries, and spread your wings, light as a feather, so you can toward the sky.

THE VOICE

Free, reborn, and proud!

The only thing keeping you from success is *YOU!* You need to spend days talking to yourself! To reach the point at which you feel it with every cell of your body, when you know you're ready for the next stage. The final breakout! When a caterpillar becomes a butterfly but not the ordinary type. There will be nothing ordinary about the Beast *you will become.* Strong, sharp, fearless, armed, dangerous! The new you, who I guarantee will be recognized by others as a superior being! Somebody to follow and learn from. You're going to capture attention everywhere you go. When you talk, others will pay attention and agree!

Now that *YOU* know who you were, are, and are about to become, we can slowly learn new ways and build that confidence.

CHAPTER 4

JOURNAL AND HOMEWORK

Journaling is a great tool in general and something I feel will be useful for you to utilize throughout the course of your journey, enabling you to not only record but also later reflect on your work and compare your knowledge and thoughts as they change parallel to your experience.

I KNOW! You're thinking, *Here we go. Just when I thought this was going to be easy, he "blanket sweeps" us with a journal and homework!*

Well, those are really just for you. Don't worry. I won't be grading you.

You won't answer to anyone but yourself. I do feel, however, that recording your thoughts and progress will help you learn from previous experiences. I've found journaling to be *VERY* useful throughout my personal journey, and I'm sure you will too.

Let's call that journal your *"ALPHA BIBLE"* if you will. And treat it as such.

Let's start with an honest, down-to-earth, cold assessment of yourself, along with your skills, abilities, and current academic and physical skill levels. Be honest here.

Nobody is going to read this but you. You don't want to start off with self-told lies, do you? It's like taking one card, bending it and making it weak, and then using it to build the foundation for the largest house of cards ever stacked! It will soon topple in shame, and you know it! Plus, the bigger you build it, the harder it will come crashing down.

Remember, the foundation is the most important part of anything you build.

So, be honest and calculated here. There's nothing to be ashamed of! You are already taking steps toward bettering yourself, and this is part of the process. Never be ashamed of who you were, but be proud of what you are about to become!

Once you do that, you can move on to the next step: goals.

I need you to set specific goals aligned with every aspect of your journey. Decide what you want to become on every level and then write those aspirations down. This is not goal-setting. Remember how we discussed setting small, attainable goals earlier? Well, what you're writing down represents the end results of your hard labor! This is what You want to be at your journey's end. Almost. That journey is actually ongoing, but one step at a time.

For now, set the standards and then follow small steps and goals toward the big picture.

We'll begin with one such goal:

Go back to school!

This should come first. Unless you already possess an academic level you are satisfied with. For those who don't, choose something you like! Something you always wanted to go for. Remember, we are not doing this for anybody but us! It's not about getting a better job or bringing a university degree home to show off! This is about accomplishing something **YOU** need so you can feel complete! Whether it be art, music, or whatever would make you feel like you've accomplished something great, take it and do it with passion!

Next on the list should be your physical assessment!

JOURNAL AND HOMEWORK

Perhaps it's human nature, but people tend to fool themselves the hardest when it comes to this. Ask yourself how others might perceive you. Are you clean and groomed enough? Do your clothes reflect who you truly are? Are you overweight? Underweight? Imagine how you would judge a person who looks like you do if you met them! Decide what your strengths are and what is holding you back!

If you have beautiful eyes, don't hide them under a lot of hair. If your teeth are pearly and straight and you have an adorable smile, use it as a tool. A weapon! If your posture makes you look like a question sign, stand up straight, for God's sake! Stand tall and confident. A "well-built figure" is a synonym for Alpha. Work on that! Join the gym and track your progress! Try to impress in every way possible.

Evaluate your vocabulary! Work on it *DAILY!* Incorporate the new words you learn in your everyday speech! And learn to recognize when opportunities come along to use them! Avoid using advanced and complicated language with those who lack the capability to understand it. This will cause discomfort and frustration in others, so choose your words wisely!

Please, and this is very important, know your grammar. Good grammar makes a big difference in the level of education you project to others. You want the perception that others have of you to be at least equal to, if not higher than, your honest opinion of yourself.

Next, I want you to visualize a realistic business goal. That could be owning a business, becoming a partner in a famous law firm, gaining the skills and education necessary to become a neurosurgeon or veterinarian, or embracing the career of an opera singer or famous painter. Whatever would make you happy to do, focus on it and write it down. Next, draw the path that will take you there. Break it down into smaller steps and then plan and execute each step with precision to get you to the next rung on the ladder!

You will need to rethink and revisit this process many, many times. Corrections and changes will happen. You may even have to redo the entire process once or twice. That's why it is so important to write it down and keep it in front of you. It's like a big puzzle. And you have to find all the pieces. But as you move forward, the more pieces you'll find and the easier it will become to fit them all in at the right times and in the right place. Remember that this is not a race. There's no clock ticking, and you don't have an exact finish line. So, pace it out, allow for mistakes and corrections, give yourself space, and you'll notice it getting easier as time goes by.

Next, I want you to log events. Mark down everything you achieve. When you get close to a goal, have another short-term goal ready to start. Write it down. Be consistent. And precise! Mark your thoughts as you go. Mark errors, pitfalls, and failures as well, and use them as learning tools. Journaling will become your best friend and trusty reference for the future.

I also want you to log anything you might encounter on your way. Any verbal argument you participate in. Win or lose. Any obstacle you must overcome. Any challenge you took on and more importantly, any ones you didn't. Because those are important to work on. Regroup, plan, and attack it again. Only this time, you'll be prepared. And you *WILL* win.

I also want you to set little tasks for yourself. Like assignments but more fun!

Go see a movie you would normally never dare to. Try something extreme. Learn to drive a standard car, motorcycle, or boat. Take up surfing, scuba diving, parachuting, sharpshooting, or whatever you would have explored had fear not held you back. Become trained in first aid. You never know when those skills might come in handy. Such experience might separate you from the crowd, make you the hero of the day, and more importantly, save a life! Try new meals, ones you are not comfortable with. Learn about different cultures and people. Visit new and exotic places. Broaden your horizons. Spend some time in a country you always wanted to visit and then one you would never have dreamed of setting foot in! Learn from everything you do

JOURNAL AND HOMEWORK

and see. Arm yourself with worldly knowledge!

Learn how to cook! Take a class! It can be so much fun and is extremely liberating!

I went to a college to become a chef! Not because I had to but because I wanted to! Educate yourself on health and fitness; learn what's good for you. Learn how to keep your body and mind healthy and clean! Take a martial arts class, which teaches you not just self-defense but also self-control, discipline, and the body-to-mind connection. You will also learn about respect.

Set a goal to read a new book every week. Choose different types and styles. Read something you normally never would!

Challenge yourself to approach that cute person in your coffee shop or gym. Practice talking to others on a regular basis. Once you grow comfortable speaking with strangers and gain more awareness of your verbal skills and broaden them, you will never have another problem expressing yourself, even with a person who intimidates you such as someone you thought was way out of your league, your boss, or a bully at the bar. Guess what? You *ARE* in that league now! You have the power! You can draw attention to yourself and voice your thoughts! You can look your boss in the eye and tell him all the ideas you've kept only in your head for so long, that you are due for that promotion and raise! Take control of your life! Once you do, people will recognize it and comply! Again, you need to prepare. Plan your approach. You can't just walk into your boss's office and demand that raise! Set an opportunity for yourself. Make your announcement at the best possible time. Be smart. Plan wisely and execute!

Ninety percent of rejected ideas don't get considered due to bad timing.

Use the same principle with everything else. And log it in the journal. Go over your notes. Learn from the past!

Here's another thing I like to do, which you can also log in your journal: Do at least one good thing every day. Be it helping an elderly person cross the street or staying calm and taking the high road when someone is having a bad day and being rude. I try to analyze the reason behind every action. If a lady at the coffee shop seems grumpy and irritated, instead of adding oil to the fire and being rude back, notice how her hair looks wonderful that morning. Respond with a smile, and you will most likely get one in return. She will then feel guilty for being rude and overcompensate with kindness. Remember—a little bit sometimes goes a long way. It can take a little nudge to push someone off a cliff, but oftentimes, an even smaller kind gesture can pull them away from it! Try to log one good deed daily in your journal. Looking back, those entries will make you smile as you reflect on all those times you were the bigger person, when you took charge of the situation and enforced your terms without the other side even knowing. Donate to charity. Every dollar I ever donated has returned to me many-fold in some form or another. Those who give, have. Remember that!

Try not to refuse to help someone whenever reasonable to do so. Remember, you are the one people others will look up to and ask for help. When you become an ALPHA, you also become responsible for those under you and need to be prepared to act anytime.

I'm not going to explain everything you can do with your journal; it's up to you to explore your limits. I just strongly suggest keeping one and logging things in it regularly. Download a journal app on your phone and type in every event, important thought, and goal as it happens or springs to mind. Then sit down when you have time and transcribe everything on that big, main paper version you keep under your bed.

I know many of you who are reading this are already thinking, *All this sounds great. I think I'll start as soon as I finish the book.* You are already excited about the prospect. Indeed, it seems like your life is already about to change as you read these pages, but I will tell you the cold truth. By the time you reach the book's end, possibly 95 percent of you will have returned to your old ways. It will be just

JOURNAL AND HOMEWORK

another New Year's resolution you didn't follow through with. And that makes me sad. I wish everyone reading this would do something to better their life and make an effort for themselves and those around them! Don't be that guy or a girl who procrastinates and never gets anything done. If there ever was a time for you to step up, it is *NOW!* What time could be better? What place is better than *HERE*? Don't wait to finish the book. Get that journal ready right away! Get going on the evaluation! Follow along with the process as you read, not after It's never too early. Neither is it ever too late. Try to understand my message, to understand how deeply you are down. How little you have lived! I know it hurts. It's hard to admit it to yourself, but the sooner you do, the sooner you can break free! Don't be afraid to leave old you behind. It wasn't good for anyone anyway! And don't be afraid to welcome New You. That You is your future best friend and ally!

Start from the beginning. And watch and track your transformation.

You will enjoy reflecting back on your first steps and following your path toward the brand-new person who will emerge from this crusty, old, boring cocoon.

What the caterpillar calls the end,
the rest of the world calls a butterfly.

—Lao Tzu

CHAPTER 5

CONFIDENCE

The journey of a thousand miles begins with one step.
—Lao Tzu

Like the rest of you, I have been taught much throughout my life. But the one thing I've been told that has possibly helped me most is to:

NEVER GIVE UP OR DOUBT MY ABILITIES!

My parents were great, and they taught me life values. I truly looked up to them and learned at an early age what's important in life, what we cannot affect, and what we need to take control of.

My dad passed away when I was seven years old, but in those short years we had together, I learned so much from him. How to be strong, to take care of your family. How to be masculine, yet gentle, kind, and loving. He transferred to me not just his love of nature, the outdoors, sports, and handiwork but also taught me about honor, valor, compassion, and a sense of justice and courage. My dad gave me more in those short years than, I think, some fathers can in a lifetime.

My brother was just a newborn baby at the time of his

passing, and though he left us too soon and too suddenly, he planted good, strong roots in my fragile young mind and set the solid foundation for my character. My mother recognized that, and over the years she watered that plant with confidence and trust in my abilities. She showed me by example how to never give up, to keep going when all seemed lost, and how to get up when life delivers a blow to your face and keep going, despite the odds against you!

"It's important to keep going," she taught me. "Get up and fight even when you think you can't!" She showed me that everything is possible while providing for the three of us and raising my brother and me to be good people. She fought for us, but she also taught us how to fight for ourselves!

My mother also showed us how to love and be loved. We learned from her empathy, sincerity, dignity, honesty, and self-sacrifice. She taught me to show emotions and be kind to others. That just because you're strong doesn't mean you should be cruel or self-centered.

She put special emphasis on honesty, punishing insincerity, and rewarding truth.

More than my father, she showed me strength as she pushed through life alone, with us two kids following in her footsteps. She never backed down or gave up. A lioness taking care of her two cubs. Every memory I have of my mom is filled with pride, love, and joy. She was my hero. The true hero among us all. A true Alpha female.

She gave me my most valuable lessons in life, and for that, I can *NEVER* thank her enough!

Was I born Alpha?!

Hardly!

I was just an average kid going with the flow and trying to fit in. But my mother sensed that I was meant for more and recognized the potential. She was feeding my personality, encouraging my spirit.

She told me constantly that I need to love myself, have confidence, and never doubt my abilities. It was she who convinced me to do a good assessment of my skills

CONFIDENCE

and capabilities and then made sure I would never doubt them again.

I wasn't always the man I am today. It was my mother who slowly planted and watered the seed of Alpha in me in my youth.

Though she was my support, my biggest fan, she was also very objective and never offered praise I didn't deserve.

As quick as she was to give positive feedback, she was realistic as well—even brutally honest at times when it came to my mistakes. She made sure to point out my errors when I made them, priming me for a future in which I could independently deal with them and fix them while overcoming any obstacles in my path in the process.

Over time, I developed a great sense of humor, captivating other's attention whenever I spoke. I became aware of the aura surrounding me. With her help, I worked on my vocabulary, learning how to express myself more effectively. Words became my toys, puzzle pieces I learned to expertly snap together as needed, and for some reason, I seemed to have a knack for putting together, clearly and concisely, whatever picture I was painting in my head!

Transferring thoughts into words is a skill I rate highly on my ladder of useful tools in life. Once you master words and grammar, and can express your thoughts as quickly as they flow into your consciousness, you become very convincing. Then you can speak with confidence, and that captures the notice of others.

My leadership skills developed as I grew, and I became one to look up to when school projects were in order. Other students would flock to me for advice, and teachers were quick to reward my newfound confidence and initiative! I started getting attention from the opposite sex, which was my first lesson in this whole Alpha thing! A key point to keep in mind: There's more than one way to be noticed; intelligence, a captivating spirit, charisma, and a confident attitude are just a few of those. Well, catching the eye of the opposite sex only boosted my confidence and made me wonder how else

I could better myself and bring out the best in me.

I eventually signed up with a local gym at age sixteen (I remember how I just couldn't wait for that birthday since sixteen was the minimum age requirement at the time), and I haven't stopped training since! It's been thirty-three-plus long years, but I have found that from a strong body and mind comes a strong spirit. Every day, I come out of the gym refreshed and ready for life's challenges! In making a point to exercise every day, I've made myself look the way I felt.

Confident and great!

I'm not the first person to unlock that secret to success. You know who did it first? Arnold Schwarzenegger! Even if you never watch television or know nothing about bodybuilding, you have still heard of this man! He started as a kid interested in bodybuilding, and with nothing but determination and sheer willpower, managed to work his way slowly up, competition by competition, until ultimately coming to America, winning seven Mr. Olympia titles and even going on to become a famous actor when his English vocabulary was shorter than the list of ingredients on a cereal box. Did that or any other obstacle stop him?

HELL, NO!

It made him want it more! And the more people laughed and mocked him, the more he kept pushing forward, confident, standing straight, and flexing those big, hard-earned muscles. And while so many were still busy making fun of his accent, stating how he was just a dumb actor with a big body and no brains, he became the governor of California. That shut everybody up in a hurry! Did you know he was once Chairman of the President's Council on Physical Fitness and Sports during George Bush Senior's term in presidency? You'll find George Bush's statement on The American Presidency Project website, which indicates that he feels Arnold to be "uniquely qualified to address and influence national health and fitness issues, especially among our youth."

You can read more on Arnold Schwarzenegger's

appointment here:
https://www.presidency.ucsb.edu/documents/statement-the-appointment-arnold-schwarzenegger-chairman-the-presidents-council-physical.

Or participated voluntarily as a donor, guest and spokesperson in the Special Olympic Games? Or host and president of the biggest show and expo fitness industry ever created: Arnold Classic? That expo, held annually, grosses millions in profit! If you didn't know that, now you do! And if you did, you just proved how big Arnold's legacy still is to this day!

The man is living proof of that Ultimate Alpha I mentioned before.

Can we all become Arnold? Not likely.

But can we try to be the best "us" we can and take advantage of our best qualities for our personal good?

Be SURE of that!

Being an Alpha in today's society means being successful in everything you do! That includes business, the sport(s) you play, romance, or just being a good parent to your children. Alphas don't know the meaning of the word **"CAN'T!"**

There's **"CAN,"** and then there's ***"We'll make it work!"***

Working out and learning from great people in the bodybuilding community made me realize some very important things, which I list below. We'll start with a big one:

Nothing is impossible.

You'll find plenty of stories in the bodybuilding world of people who, through incredibly hard work, overcame the strong genetics of others standing with them on the competitive stage. Through sheer dedication, willpower, and discipline, they achieved the goals they envisioned.

Lou Ferrigno didn't let his disability (80 percent hearing loss) stop him from achieving greatness. In fact, I believe he did this despite it.

Hard work, discipline, and ethics always pay dividends in the long run.

That old story "The Hare and the Tortoise" serves as a good example of this. The latter kept going at its typical slow pace, but it did so with determination and consistency, though it knew it could not compete with the hare's speed. The tortoise never stopped, never gave up. And eventually, it won the race against the hare, who greatly underestimated its opponent and grew so sure of its success that it stopped for long breaks. This story has another valuable lesson beyond that of not giving up. Did you pick up on it? Here it is:

NEVER underestimate others. Especially if you're in competition with them. Also, don't overestimate your own abilities. But we'll talk more on this later in the text.

I like to say: "Even if you're moving at a snail's pace, you're doing more than just sitting on the couch!"

Consistency is the key to success.

If you give 100 percent *ALL* the time, day in and day out, not every other day or when you feel like it. If you do this *EVERY DAY*, there's no way you won't achieve your goals.

Setting goals and following through with your plan is essential.

It is VERY important to have a plan and then follow it. Set goals, write them down, and reflect on them often, thinking of ways to better meet them.

To really start believing in yourself and your abilities, you need to first sit down and take a hard and long look at yourself and admit what your weaknesses are. Just as crucially, you must realize your strengths. Being Alpha isn't about being perfect in one or two things. It's about being versatile and very good in all the things you do! This takes time and practice, and it certainly doesn't happen overnight. The process is hard and painful, but always keep in mind that ultimate goal. Even if you get to live ten years as a Lion (an Alpha Lion), it's better than spending the rest of your life living under a rock in fear, like you are doing currently. Yes! Fear! It is my Alpha right to call you out on that, and your New Alpha-in-Training has a duty to accept that fact! Let's make peace with that and move on, shall we?

CONFIDENCE

It matters not who you were but who you are about to become, so suck it up, and let's do this!

Let's talk about one of the first steps that really trips people up: gaining self-confidence.

Why is this so hard?

Well, to answer that, I'm going to have to step into some murky waters, make some waves, but the Alpha in me says that it's necessary, so I'm plunging ahead. Jump in with me, and let's go!

We live in a highly developed society. I was originally born and raised in Europe. In Yugoslavia. Then it fell apart and became Serbia. I'm proud of my heritage and wouldn't change it for anything in this world. I was already older when I moved to North America, and my Alpha personality was already developed. I had twenty-five years of life experience under my belt, survived three wars, spent time in army service, got married, fathered my first child, and everything else you could and couldn't imagine in between.

When I started my new life in Canada, back in 1999, I noticed one thing. People were very different here. At first I didn't understand why. But over the years I found the problem. Yes. Let's call it what it is.

People here believe us Serbians to not be exactly what you call *NORMAL!* I noticed we were different too. They call us loud, obnoxious, headstrong, quick to act! Many people actually fear us without even getting to know us. It took me years to understand this phenomenon, but then I finally got to the bottom of it! I realized there are a lot more Alpha Serbians than North Americans (and I've been all over the US and Canada alike). Not that I'm trying to put anybody down. Please, that is not my intention at all!

Remember, I'm trying to help you become your better self!

I'm on your side!

But ask any honest person whether they want some Serbian friends around when the soup gets thick, and I'm sure they would all agree on the answer!

OMEGA TO ALPHA

So *WHY IS THAT,* you're probably wondering!

Serbians live in a very different society. I won't go into too much detail about how I grew up, but living in poor conditions, with an economy that almost joined the dinosaurs in their extinction—not to mention the war that swept through the country that lasted twelve-plus long years—one would expect us to be low-drive, dead-spirited, and submissive people.

But that didn't happen.

Quite the opposite, in fact.

It would seem that a hard life, and being forced to deal with problems from a young age, actually develops your personality and makes you more resilient, strong, resourceful, and witty. It teaches you how to fight, to resist.

It teaches you how to survive.

"Hard times create strong men, strong men create good times, good times create weak men, weak men create hard times."

This is the line from the novel *Those Who Remain* by G. Michael Hopf.

I soon realized that what had happened over there was not nearly as bad as what is happening to people here. And I can see it because I'm an outsider! Like watching a chess match and seeing all the right moves, though both players are oblivious to them!

North American society intentionally killed the Alpha in you. No joke! Systematically, slowly but surely, everything in this society is designed to "Tame the Lion!" From a young age, you are taught about rules. How to behave. To keep your head down.

Don't talk back and ask questions. In school, you can't question your grades. Can't challenge teachers to prove you know more. If you want to continue your education, the cost is so high that you are forced to obtain a loan, which they so generously and readily give to you so you can achieve the academic level you desire. You are forced to work through your college years to support yourself until you graduate with your degree and get a job. But now you are part of the big machine! You need to keep your head down because you can't risk losing your job! How will you ever pay off that loan otherwise? So, you sit there and work, burying yourself deeper in debt as you struggle with a car loan, credit cards, bills, and a mortgage or rent payments! You become a hamster, running and spinning that wheel forever, getting nowhere while life goes by like a speeding train, moving so fast, you couldn't board it even if you wanted to! Hours, days, and years of your life pass by until you can't help but ask whether you ever really lived or if it was all just a dream.

Sound familiar yet?

And society is designed to make a zombie out of you. Of us!

Because guess what?!

It's run by Alpha people who don't need more Alphas to challenge them, making ripples and waves on the calm surface! They want everything for themselves! They've used their Alpha brains to design machinery that run on Omega fuel, feeding you fear, insecurity, and low self-esteem. They've set up society to make you feel like a maggot, forcing you to wiggle and get by only existing! They want you locked down and quiet inside a prison of fear, doubt, and problems, away from ever seeing the truth.

The truth that you're *WORTH IT!* That you can be **ALPHA** too! That you have it in you! That it's screaming inside of you, waiting to be unleashed!! Do you feel it? That feeling you get when in the movies good guys win and justice prevails? In your stomach, like butterflies, only much better, stronger?

That's the **ALPHA** wanting to get out! Let it and be rid of misery once and for all! For your own good and the good of everyone around you!

Okay, let's circle back to the topic of *CONFIDENCE*.

It isn't something you are born with but what you can gain and build during your lifetime. You can also lose it, and much faster, than gain it. Because we humans are very fragile and self-conscious creatures. At least most of us are.

Truth is, only you are responsible for your confidence level and its preservation! Never let anybody take it from you!

Self-esteem and Self-worth are both determined by YOU. No one else can define those values but you.

You know those people, and we've all met some examples at some point, who just seem naturally attractive to the opposite sex and also capture the attention of the same sex? Those individuals whom you can't stop listening to and laugh at all their jokes? If you think about it, they might not be so physically attractive—in fact, sometimes they're not at all—yet they seem to exude a kind of charisma, an aura of charm and positive energy that make you and the rest of the room gravitate in their direction. I'm not talking about stand-up comedians or motivational speakers, although they have the right idea. I'm talking about everyday people you see at work, coffee places you have your lunch at, supermarkets, or school.

Those are Alphas. Consciously or not, they are demonstrating their confidence and charm, and others can't help but notice! You see young, beautiful women in the company of short, balding, older gentlemen, or the opposite: successful, middle-aged businesswomen in the company of young guys, and you automatically think, *MONEY TALKS!*

That isn't always necessarily the case. On the other hand, if that gentleman has money and is successful and well-rounded in everything he does, isn't that an example of the things I'm trying to teach you here? Isn't he an Alpha and therefore attractive to that fine, young female specimen? Isn't money irrelevant?

We are quick to judge, to blame others for our failure and attribute their successes to luck and chance.

But think about it. You can be that person too. You just need to bring yourself up to that level.

But we need to start small first.

One more thing before we continue.

Remember how I said we are our worst enemy? Well, again, in this case, we have to take care not to fall into the trap of sabotaging our success.

"Why would I want to do that now, after I already killed the Voice and Omega two chapters ago?" you might ask.

Well, trying to achieve your goals too fast can also trigger your downfall. You need to take a slow approach and really work on building a strong foundation for future Super You.

I will assume you already did a self-evaluation and decided what your strengths were and what things you need to work on, so I'm going to move forward with the next step and teach you how to get that confidence that is **SO** important on your new journey. It takes practice, but then, nothing worth having comes overnight!

When I say don't try to get there too fast, I mean:
Do not try to trick yourself into being too confident!

It's a very common trap, primitive and simple, yet it goes really deep. Should you fall into it, all your hard work will need to be redone, and you will have to start from ground zero again!

I mentioned Imaginary Alpha at the beginning. It's easy to fall under the assumption that you have confidence. A lot of people wear that costume every day. You know a few of them too, might even be one of them. They are semi-successful, semi-good at charming the opposite sex, and usually loud in crowds to ensure the attention is fixed on them. Those are the ones willing to walk over dead bodies to succeed! But don't let that facade fool you! Deep inside they are battling their own insecurities and fears and are walking, ticking time bombs because, at their first encounter with a real Alpha, they'll topple like a house of cards. They know it because they get tested *EVERY* day out there, and every time they do, they fail! Often, they'll attempt to make their appearance intimidating, depending on what part of the world they roam in. Business types will wear sharp suits and expensive watches, drive overpriced cars he or she can barely afford, and go out of their way to ensure that everything you see on the outside is perfect, even when their rent is half their car payment. In their closet, there are two suits and four shirts for mix-and-match. They eat cereal for breakfast but always have lunch at that expensive restaurant across the street from their workplace, usually with their boss. They eat microwave dinners at home, pay their utility bills late, and are hounded by collection agencies over their maxed-out credit cards.

In lower-standing parts of society, those types usually come in the form of tough-looking folks with lots of tattoos, driving some kind of muscle car or loud motorcycle to attract attention.

I've even encountered Imaginary Alphas who cut themselves to have scars, a sure testament to their toughness, right?

No matter at which level of society you encounter such individuals, you can expose them with a simple test!

Look them in the eye! Imaginary Alphas will not be able to withstand a true, honest, piercing gaze from a true one! Exceptions to this rule are very rare! They will challenge you, make you sweat a little and even doubt yourself, but eventually, they'll be the ones to look away, which, in the animal kingdom, means the ultimate surrender! After it happens once, they won't challenge you again! You can be sure of that! That type doesn't like to lose.

I'm not completely against a "fake it until you make it" life hack in this regard, but use it wisely.

Why is this so important?! Think about it! When you go for a job interview, the boss or manager in charge will be impressed if you look straight into their eyes while you talk. This projects confidence and sincerity. Women often say the first thing they notice in a man is their eyes! Coincidence? I don't think so. They are simply more attracted to guys who can look them in the eyes and pass that ultimate test! That means you have nothing to hide, that you are confident, open, and trustworthy. You stand erectly, shoulders square, welcoming challenges, friendship, romance, or responsibility! You are going to take care of business and do it to the best of your abilities! That's what people see in

Alphas. Most of the time others are unaware of this fact, but there's no reason you shouldn't be! And take advantage of that knowledge. That is how you will become successful, how you will capture the attention of others in the future and make them trust and follow you.

Another good example of this particular phenomenon can be found in the men and women who train salespeople. This person has mastered the art of conversation and manipulation. They can convince you of anything they want you to believe. They'll summarily beat down every argument you present against their product, and you will end up buying it at the end, even after you promised yourself you wouldn't at the beginning of the presentation! There are two other, obvious types who share those skills. Politicians and lawyers! They can argue until you can't think of one more objective and talk for hours on a topic while saying very little or nothing.

These people are dangerous.

And their secret is *TRAINING!*

They have been trained long and hard on how to do what they do best! They've become masters of that skill! And guess what?

Their training is based on the same rules we are deploying here.

You'd better believe it.

Through the lessons described in this book, you will be trained in ALL aspects of life, not just body language, conversational skills, and eye contact! You must adopt those rules and not act/fake them but actually *LIVE* by them! I've broken down the process of gaining confidence into these three steps below, starting with:

1. Practice.

Repetition is the key!

Teach yourself to walk tall and straight and be sure to maintain the correct posture with each step! Widen your shoulders. Open up to people when you talk to them. Practice eye contact. Of course, do not go to extremes, such as walking into a bar with twenty Hell's Angels and staring them all down for five minutes! That just might get you hurt. But practice on regular people, and build up to meeting the eyes of those who intimidated you when you were still afraid. That Omega. The best way to overcome our fears is to face them!

Courage is not the absence of fear but rather the ability to control it!

That's what this part is all about! Go out and practice! Walk up to that big muscle-head in the gym who took your equipment while you were getting a drink of water, look him in the eyes, stand tall, and say calmly that you were using that particular machine and weren't done with it. He will have no choice but to apologize and let you share the equipment. Don't come in rude and hot; that might trigger the opposite reaction, and you might end up in the hospital. But if you have your posture right, make eye contact, and calmly state what he needs to hear, I guarantee you, he will back down. He will realize that he's the one who is wrong in this and compensate for that with kindness.

If you see that hot one at the club, the one you've always liked but thought was way out of your league, approach them and strike up a conversation. Again, be confident and secure. Strong voice, direct eye contact, charming smile, and a good line. People like confidence, and they can sense it. Even if you don't get their phone number, you got noticed. They know who you are now. And it's good practice for future encounters.

2. Moderation!

Don't let people mistake your confidence for cockiness. It's easy to cross that line if you flirt with it, but it's also necessary to perfect it. You'll get it eventually. Don't worry!

As you practice, stay consistent and practice moderation

in how you present your new and improved, confident self. Put yourself to the tests and learn from them. Do things you wouldn't have dared before, and see how it helps you evolve.

3. Appearance.

It is essential that you work on your appearance. You need to look the way you feel.

Remember how we said at the beginning that in the animal world, the Alpha is the strongest, fittest, and most skillful in the pack? Well, just go by that and ratchet your physical appearance up a few notches! If you can will yourself to become more educated, sophisticated, secure, and charming, improving the physical part of the equation shouldn't be a problem at all. You just need to advance your fitness level to some degree. You can choose to build muscle and become a bigger version of yourself or go the conditioning route and become fit and tight.

You can take martial arts, advancing to a level at which you can defend yourself and others. I will let you choose the level and type of physical form you want to claim for yourself.

But what I'm not going to give you a choice on is your personal hygiene! To look good, you *NEED* to be clean. To look sharp. That is the second thing people look for after establishing eye contact! Let's face it; we all can't have Brad Pitt's face, but you can certainly work with what you have and bring it up to your best.

Let's look at some basic areas you can easily improve upon to make a big impact.

Hair. Do something funky! Leave an impression. If you are balding, please, for the love of everything good in this world, do not go for the dreaded comb-over, that is, growing your hair on one side and then covering your bald spot with it. I said *WORK* with what you have, not *HIDE* it! If you are balding and can't afford a hair transplant or hair-growth products, shave your head*!* Believe me, you will look much better, cleaner, and sharper. And more confident! You would be surprised by how many people react positively to a shaved head. I should know (although I shave it by choice).

Teeth. Yours must be clean and white*!* Your smile is the second thing people notice after your eyes! Many people's top pet peeve is bad breath! So, brush often, rinse in between, and keep a pack of gum handy at all times. Bad breath, for many, is a dealbreaker!

Glasses. If you must wear them, opt for those designer frames that go with your face type. Let experts choose one that makes you look good. Or wear contacts if you don't feel comfortable with glasses. Get surgery if it's in your budget. Whichever choice offers you the most satisfying result.

Clothes. I will leave this category up to you. Wear something that compliments your body type. Whether you are overweight or skinny, tall or short, pick something that plays to your strengths. Dress for the body you have, not the one you desire. There will be time for that once you sculpt yourself into that fit New You. Don't wear clothes that are too conservative. Remember, you want to appear open to people and easily accessible! Keep that in mind! Don't look too eccentric!

The goal here is to make YOU feel comfortable. You will **NEVER** feel confident by **NOT** being you and not liking yourself or your appearance! So, mainly dress and do things for yourself, but keep in mind not to go overboard, and try to look appealing to others as well!

Now that we have you all dressed and looking good, remember that a smile goes a long way, and always speak calmly and convincingly while making eye contact!

One more thing that I would like to stress, although this should automatically improve with a higher level of education, is your *VOCABULARY!*

I have a friend who decided at one point to learn a new word every day!

Now, he didn't just learn new words just for the sake of knowing them. He learned new words to properly use them in daily conversation! Little by little, his vocabulary

CONFIDENCE

has broadened, and now, when he speaks to someone, he leaves the impression on that person that they are speaking with someone who surely teaches English at college!

It took a little effort on a daily basis yet made an enormous improvement in the long run!

That is what I meant by not rushing to become superior! Give it time. Perform small tasks toward that goal. And it will creep up on you one day and take you by surprise how much you prospered! Be sure to perform these tasks often. And your success will be inevitable!

To sum it all up, do what you feel is necessary to excel in everything. Take your time and arm yourself not just with patience but also mes with discipline and consistency. Put in the work day in and day out. Even small steps count. Try to move forward every day, even if it's only by one baby step.

When I let go of what I am, I become what I might be.

—Lao Tzu

And remember!
YOU have the power!

CHAPTER 6

POWER

Lao Tzu once said, "He who controls others may be powerful, but he who has mastered himself is mightier still."

In this chapter, I would like to talk about one very important thing.

Power!

We need to touch basis on few facts that will be important in understanding power, obtaining it and utilizing it in every day life.

What is POWER?

As I mentioned, there are many ways to be powerful. At this point, you may be wondering, what is **POWER** really?!

The definition of power in a crossword puzzle is: *The ability to do something or act in a particular way.*

I like to believe that true power comes with having mastery over oneself. Of one's emotions and actions!

Once you gain full control over yourself, how you express yourself and act, people will recognize this ability in you and see you as a person they can learn from and willingly follow.

That's the first step in your journey!

When I say power I'm talking about its use in many forms and ways. The power to control yourself, to maintain composure under pressure and when times call for action, and to control others, steering them away from wrong-doings, arguments, and even physical fights. The power to speak the truth and instill trust in others when you do. The power to change things and lives, your own and that of those around you.

Your first glimpse of power came when you took control over your life, started reading this book, and decided to will yourself into making a change! By taking that step, you gained a new bar on the power level meter, and now, there's no going back! You must feel rejuvenated, a little different. You've made the BIGGEST decision of your life thus far.

I know it's scary. Your knees feel weak, your heart is racing, and breathing is an effort, but you must also feel lighter, free of the chains and bonds, like inhaling fresh air, feeling blood rushing through your veins. That's the power I'm talking about. From this moment on, you will become more powerful with every step you take on your new, lasting journey. I promise you that. Even when times get tough, even if you face doubt at some point, remember, it is all part of your evolution and progress. Don't forget that sometimes we need to take a step back to move forward. Just keep that in mind, arm yourself with patience, and build this masterpiece one little segment at a time!

If you look at successful people, no matter which aspect of life they've succeeded in, you'll discover that they all found a way to overpower their competition. They became the best at what they do, be that sports, politics, business, peacemaking, or science. They all played to their strengths and won!

Broaden your skill set.

Imagine if you could apply the same theory to everything you do in life. Play to your strengths. But before you can do that, you must widen your strength spectrum! Become strong in all aspects of life. Education, physical strength, verbal skills, love life, music, knowledge of food, seduction, investing, martial arts, languages... The possibilities are endless, and so is the time you have to master them!

Whatever you are already strong at, polish it to perfection. Let that be your base!

Then work on the rest of your skills slowly and gradually!

Do what you love.

Get that job you've always wanted! Even if, at first, it doesn't pay as much as your old one! Doing something you love will ensure fast progress in your workplace and a salary to follow!

Think about it. Your work is something you will be putting your time and effort into all your life, where you will devote most of your time. So why not do something you really enjoy?

I feel that doing what you love, among a few other things, is the key to happiness.

Surround yourself with positive and supportive people.

Embrace the company of like-minded people! Your friends and family can help **SO** much if guided properly! But...

They can also hold you back. Negative people are very dangerous to others. I call them Energy Leaches. They can suck the life force and positivity right out of you.

If negative people start doubting and slowing you down, get rid of them!

Believe me, it's better to leave a non-supportive friend/spouse than to suffer due to their incompetence and pessimism!

Many times, I've seen talented people allow their potential to go unfulfilled because of others in their lives.

New You needs new things and positive surroundings, and people are very important in this process! If someone wants to jump on your train for a free ride, by all means, let them, but if that person's an emergency brake-puller, to hell with them! They can go and run themselves down with misery. Do not let them stop you on your new path!

Help yourself—only then can you help others.

One important thing I want to mention here, and I *can't stress it enough:*

DO NOT TRY TO CHANGE THE WORLD... JUST YOURSELF!

And I mean it. Let me explain this in a little more detail.

While trying to help others is noble and great—and very tempting, I might add—it will only slow you down, wasting precious energy that you need for your journey! Once you become New You, once you are an Alpha, by all means, go out and help as many people as you want to reach their full potential! Look at me. I'm writing a book for God's sake! But only after you reach your final destination. Not sooner. Trust me, you will thank me later. Think back to every flight you've taken. While in your seat, waiting for takeoff, a flight attendant always steps over to the front of the aisle and demonstrates how to act in the case of an emergency. Do you recall how that attendant always says to put the oxygen mask on your face FIRST, then your child, even while all your instincts are screaming at you to do the opposite?! Well, think about it. That's kind of how this works! How are you supposed to help others without helping yourself first?!

Power is drawn to power.

You know how, when lightning strikes near a house, it affects all the nearby power lines nearby? How it connects to other sources of power wirelessly? That is the phenomenon I'm talking about here. You will see how, as you gain power, you start to attract other powerful people around you. You will find it easier to work with other Alphas too. Another glitch in nature's plan! In the animal world, Alphas fight automatically, as I said, often to the death. With humans, it works a little differently. Naturally, there can **ONLY** be one top dog, but many Alphas in a human pack can work together, making that pack better, stronger, and ultimately, almost unstoppable. People use reason and tolerate each other because they are capable of focusing on a greater cause, the ultimate goal. In a society where Alphas are equal, Omegas are few, and everybody prospers and has everything they need!

It is a distant, somewhat unrealistic goal, but we are not here to change or better the world! I'm just working to better one person at the time! The rest is up to you!

You need to learn to gain power, then control it. You will learn your own way to obtain more of it. Whether that be pursuing education, joining the gym, learning a new language or skill, or working on your charm and social skills. I'm only giving you the tools. The rest is up to you.

I'm going to end this chapter on a very crucial point. You take it with you and keep it close!!

Strive for perfection.

Whatever you decide to do, whatever you need to work on and better yourself at, go into it with a positive attitude and 110 percent devotion!

You *MUST* give it your all and do the *BEST* you possibly can if you want to succeed!

We've already killed the Old You, the you who would have settled for another 85 percent on a test or finishing third in a race. New You needs near perfection! If you fail, do it again. If you barely pass, do it again! When you are done with it, you'd better be a NEAR expert in what you've learned! And I mean it! For your own good!

Look at me! An immigrant who could barely speak English twenty-plus years ago, writing a book!

And you are reading it!

You think I didn't have doubts? That I didn't have

haters and doubters telling me to just give up, that I would never finish this book, let alone publish it? You know what I said to them?

Nothing! *That's right!* **Big Fat Nothing!**

Because I know better than to listen to the miserable little souls who find comfort after their failures by laughing at others' attempts at greatness! Those are Omegas and always will be. Unless they read this book, which I doubt! I've trained myself to not let things like that affect my judgment or confidence! So can you! I promise you that!

Just think about it! You sit EVERY day in front of a TV or game console; you read a good book or drink coffee and gossip with your friends, all while life is passing you by. Those are hours of your life you will never get back! We've invented a million ways to make time go by faster, but nothing to slow it down or stop it! You know what slows down time?

SUCCESS!

That's right! Once you get there, you can stop and smell all the roses you want... And jasmines... And lilies...

You get my point! Work hard to get there, then set the cruise control and enjoy life! At the top of the food chain! Surrounded by people who think alike and have time to join you!

Always remember that with great power comes great responsibility! Don't ever abuse the power and control you'll find you have over others at times. Use these tools to become a better you. Not for personal gain or exploitation. By growing into all you can be, money will come inevitably, but that true treasure—the true miracle—is that person you've become! Never forget that!

CHAPTER 7

RESPONSIBILITIES

We're going to circle back to something I mentioned at the end of the last chapter: With great power comes great responsibility. You may have heard this nugget of wisdom in a *Spiderman* movie or two, or maybe somewhere else, but it's true. Once you master that power and confidence, you'll find that it comes with a great deal of responsibility! Never take that for granted. Always remember where you came from and why you started this journey! You will never fully complete the circle if you start the process with a selfish agenda. You know those people who supported you on your journey? They are very important for the final outcome. What's more important is that you don't forget to give back to those same people who stuck by your side and believed in you. Even during those times when you lacked confidence and hope!

The Alpha is a dominant, strong leader. But the Real Alpha must be like that for all who depend on and follow him/her! In the animal world, that means they must provide food, security, and a good home to the dependable members of their community. The same rules apply in our world. You must care for those who support, care for, and love you.

As I've said, an Imaginary Alpha will walk over everybody and everything to get where they're headed, following the belief that the *end justifies means*

You must never be like that. If you are, then you have learned nothing from me, and God be with you.

Being an Alpha doesn't mean that you are independent, that you need no one in your life and can now laugh at your inferiors and despise them. As mentioned, you have a part to play in your community and in society, and it's crucial. You should help others once you reach the final stage of your transformation, and I truly mean it! It is your duty. Your responsibility! In doing so, you will provide not only more personal growth and satisfaction for yourself but also for those around you! You will discover that helping others makes you stronger. You'll derive power from every good deed you unselfishly do. Everything that you give, you'll get back many-fold. That is the beauty of having the privilege to help! The strong help others grow stronger. And in the long run, you will realize that you've set a solid foundation to further empower the strong pack you have created around you! As you pass your knowledge onto others, you build the ultimate big picture! The sooner you teach your children these same rules and life truths, the sooner they will become strong pillars of your empire and ensure a bright future for you and them alike, guaranteeing that your legacy will live on long after you are gone!

It's not how long we get to spend on this Earth, but rather what we do with that time given to us!

—Dejan Garalejic

I feel I can't fully take credit for this quote because I've borrowed a few things I've heard people say on this topic for the book. I've put those thoughts together, compiling

RESPONSIBILITIES

them within these pages, and have added some of my own, so there it is. Take it to heart because it's very true.

What will people remember about you after you are gone? Will they take what you've taught them and pass it on? Or will they forget you soon after you've passed? Maybe you think it won't matter once you're gone, but believe me when I say this: If you did everything right and became what we are trying to achieve here, long after your spirit leaves this world, people will remember you. Everyone whose life you've touched WILL remember you, and those people will tell stories and carry good memories inside them for a long time!

History does remember the tyrants, but the best stories are told about heroes, about courage and beating the odds! Books are written and movies are made about those who never gave up when times got tough, about the few facing the many, about those who demonstrated superhuman strength, will, and courage and single-handedly changed the course of history. And more importantly, the lives of others! Think about that.

So be responsible and always think before you act. Plan ahead, develop a strategy, and follow it. Be prepared. Remain aware of the world around you. Keep one eye open because people like you draw a lot of attention, and some of that attention will be negative. You will encounter enemies in many forms and will need to train yourself to recognize and neutralize them at an early stage. Because the mightier you become, the stronger and in greater numbers they will appear!

Not to worry. I actually welcome my enemies and am not afraid to tell them, "Bring it on for I will be ready when you do! Having you helps me remember who I am and ensures that I'm always prepared!"

Sometimes, being an Alpha, you will find yourself growing lazy and lethargic. Oblivious to the dangers that might be waiting! Having enemies keeps you alert and on your toes! Just be sure to develop the skills necessary to recognize them and keep them at bay!

For your own good.

CHAPTER 8:

OBSERVATION (ENEMIES, FRIENDS, AND EVERYTHING IN BETWEEN)

You'll find a lot to watch out for once you reach your Alpha status. But even before that, you'll need to stay alert for anything that could slow you down or even sidetrack you on your journey to becoming better, stronger, and faster! I've accumulated a list of the most common roadblocks below to help prepare you. That way, you'll recognize those things/people as soon as they rear their heads, a good step toward helping you protect yourself and your investment!

Yourself

This may surprise you, but yes, the biggest enemy to watch out for by far is *YOU!*

We tend to keep ourselves from reaching goals, talk ourselves down and away from the challenge and potential danger, question every move we are about to make, and in general, do whatever it takes to keep us in that glass sphere, safe and sound, surviving this life as it ticks by.

To stand on the sidelines, sheltered from a potential failure by not even trying, not making the effort, never reaching beyond the safe zone to try something new, something uncertain—and something necessary to ultimately succeed!

This will be your downfall if you let your old instincts guide your future. Instead, follow my suggestions and take those steps. Throw away those doubts and old clichés, all the molds that others have made to make a so-called perfect specimen out of you! Not perfect for your advantage but for theirs, allowing them to gain easier control over you, remotely making every move for you, turning you into that perfect hamster in that perfect wheel, harvesting most of the energy you produce while spinning it!

It's a big mechanism, carefully designed and camouflaged to ensure you remain blissfully unaware of its existence. We are all slaves to a few Alpha people! Billions of people serve and obey a few! Those are the ones behind the curtains, the ones who answer to nobody! Much of humanity slaves day and night under their iron-fisted rule. We supply energy and money to them daily, feeding their power and greed at the cost of our freedom and health! We may not be aware of it, but that's how they designed the system! They appoint national presidents; decide where the next war will take place, who will be involved in it, and who will win or lose; dictate all the laws in this world; and are so powerful that any attempt to bring them down yields only one outcome. The one we don't want to accept as an option! Failure. So, I just want to say that we are not here to create world peace. Nor are we here to fight those Puppet Masters holding the strings, who are high in the food chain.

That would be silly and self-destructive! And I, being an Alpha and knowing my abilities, have made peace with that! I can't change the system, but I can teach you how to adapt to it and make a better place for yourself in it! Now, if you decide that it's in you to fight those who oppress us, by all means, do so! That's your decision, and I won't judge you!

But one day, during my early childhood, while reading

OBSERVATION (ENEMIES, FRIENDS, AND EVERYTHING IN BETWEEN)

that classic novel *Don Quixote* by Miguel de Cervantes, I decided that I would not go charging at proverbial windmills on my journey, no matter how noble that might seem. I realized the truth of the matter: that it would just be a waste of energy and time. Something left for fools to try!

For those who didn't read the book, here's the abridged version: Don Quixote, a self-proclaimed Spanish hero, set out to save the world. Sadly, for all his good intentions, Don Quixote's exploits lived only in his mind. He charged windmills, perceiving them as monsters who needed to be slain.

He was courageous and chivalrous, though a fool and perhaps a man suffering from an acute mental illness as he was shown to be delusional. As much as I loved him as a character, I knew that in real life, we need to focus on REAL goals and be able to distinguish those from the "windmills" around us that are mere distractions.

We have a more important agenda here and must focus our energy toward achieving that goal! No time for foolish ideals and dreams!

Part of becoming an Alpha means you must evaluate your abilities and use them wisely. That includes avoiding battles you can't possibly win. Instead, you should preserve that energy for other challenges, those that you can carefully prepare for and engage with on your turf and by your rules! In life, before diving into a conflict, you must ensure you have every possible advantage you can get and be sure of your victory before the battle even begins!

So, again, do not dream of making the world a better place. That battle is already lost. Rather, try to make yourself the best you can possibly be to take advantage of everything that this world, the way it is, has to offer!

The things you must watch for are many when it comes to grappling with yourself as an enemy, though most such issues, I trust you can deal with on your own.

For the sake of this top category on the checklist (Yourself), I'm just pointing out the most extreme examples.

But I will say it again and will never tire of repeating it.
You really need to watch for yourself!
NEVER forget who you are and why are you doing this!
Keep your head in check and don't grow lazy or over-confident. Don't get cozy or feel too safe and let the enemy sneak too close! That's why they use drills in the army! To keep soldiers alert all the time! And you never know whether it's a drill or the real thing in the service, so you have to train yourself to react either way!
That is the number one thing to watch for because that is the mother of all mistakes you can make!

Old Alphas

Another thing you need to watch for is Old Alphas.
They will recognize you.
They might come in the form of your current boss, whose office you have eyes on now, or that big guy in the gym everybody lets get away with things, or that handsome guy dating the girl you set out to charm and seduce...
All those are your enemies. You need to keep an eye on what they do and how they react to New You!
You'll start to get noticed. People around you will grow aware of the changes you are going through.
Most will like what they see as people tend to gravitate toward strong personalities and leadership skills. Many will try to get on your good side, but beware! Some will shift their mood the other way as randomly as the wind blows, and chances are, they have already formed an alliance with that other Alpha you set your energy on! So, be careful what you say and in front of whom you say it! Take such measures when choosing friends and allies as well, for you can truly trust no one but yourself. Some people are good to have by your side. Some will help you out of loyalty, but true friends are few. Keep those close to you, but also, and I can't stress this enough, keep a close eye on them! The Alpha in them might decide it's their time and do whatever it takes to

OBSERVATION (ENEMIES, FRIENDS, AND EVERYTHING IN BETWEEN)

take control!

Old Alphas won't go down without a fight; it's just a simple law of nature.

One you can always count on!

So, before you try to dethrone or jump over an Old Alpha, make sure you've got a solid game plan. Ensure there are no gaps or room for failure! Once everything is in place, execute your strategy flawlessly. If you can accomplish this, even an Old Alpha will be glad he passed the baton to a superior specimen! He can finally relax and stop looking over his shoulder. Most likely, he'll even become your friend and ally! It was his duty to defend his position. Since he no longer has that need, he can accept the new order and go with it! You should also show respect toward your opponent, honor him for his efforts and for the path he created for your future advancement, and keep him close and high in the ranks! He still has a few fights in him, and you want those to happen by your side with him as your ally!

And that is another thing to watch for!

In this life, real friends are few... Moreover, it is *VERY* hard to create new friendships!

Think about it! Every time you create a new enemy, you lose *DOUBLE!* You've missed an opportunity to make a friend and created an enemy instead! Do you now see what I mean!? Choose your friends wisely, as I mentioned, but even more so, take great care in choosing your enemies! They are *EASY* to create! Remain well aware of your actions at all times and take great care in what you say and how you act because it's so easy to step over someone and their feelings. Once that's done, that person is lost forever! From that moment on, you will need to worry about them, look over your shoulder, and question the motive behind their every move! So, as a golden rule, I suggest thinking long and hard before you turn someone against you! Keep in mind, there's a way to beat people at their own game, advance, and still keep them by your side!

Then there are those miserable creatures who feed off

the misfortune of others and live their lives drowning in a sea of envy over pretty much everything that other people have, most of all, over others' success! Those Omegas who lie and conspire like weasels, living in shadows, gossiping, waiting for an opportunity to bring down someone stronger and more important than them! So twisted and deformed, they form packs, and together, they dig and scratch, looking for ways to destroy everything that is just and progressive! Like hyenas. They don't desire power or recognition! Their sole purpose is to bring about misfortune to others and derive a weird, demented sense of satisfaction from their schemes! They are everywhere, and they are weak, but beware. When they're many, even the strongest have trouble withstanding their low blows! So, and I cannot repeat this enough, *WATCH OUT!* Keep your eyes and mind open, and never get caught off guard! You may feel that the slings and arrows of Omegas are not a big issue and that Old Alphas are just as manageable, but even the smallest problem can evolve into a disaster if neglected long enough. A person who remains alert is a person who is rarely taken by surprise!

Alpha Females

Let me move on to a whole new enemy here! One you may not expect. As an Alpha, you must watch for this one, even as you may find yourself strangely attracted to her looks, smells, and charms! Arm yourself with wisdom, patience, and a heavy arsenal of weapons before taking on this challenge!

I'm talking about Alpha females!

Let's stop here for a second. I want to make something clear. I'm aware that many of my readers are likely women! I also know that in my book, the experiences I'm trying to pass on are those of a male Alpha. I need to apologize for that, but as it is, I lack knowledge of how exactly every Alpha trait functions in the female world—though gauging from my personal experience, the differences I've noticed are small and not that influential over the results. So, whatever I

OBSERVATION (ENEMIES, FRIENDS, AND EVERYTHING IN BETWEEN)

say about the Alpha Male, I believe, can transfer over to the Female Alpha as well!

Again, let me remind you that I'm merely providing the necessary tools here. Everyone's experience will be individual, and some points I'm making here might slightly differ in your case, but that's the beauty of it, you see!

You will never be exactly what I want you to become! You will be who you want and need to be! Unique and beautiful in your individuality!

So, to swing back to my original topic, to the New You, the Alpha Male, the Alpha Female might ultimately be your Achilles heel! Your doom! Or, conversely, it might be your biggest blessing!

Don't get me wrong! Not ALL Alphas will be enemies! Male or female! Some will coexist with you, as long as you don't cross boundaries and trespass into their territory!

The Female Alpha will feel compelled to become your enemy the second she sets an eye on something you have and she needs! But if you play your cards right, she might become your ultimate **PRIZE!** Remember that Pack Leader from the beginning of this story? He had the She Alpha by his side! To be complete, you need one too!

Unless you have different sexual preferences, of course! Then you know what to do, and I can't really give you advice there! I guess it's just a variation of the general rule!

Also be aware that not all She Alphas will be a match made in Heaven! Some you will have to tame! Some will be happy to be tamed while others might resist!

Note: When I say "tame," what I really mean is that she will accept you as an equal, a friend or mate. I'm not saying you need to exert dominance. Just secure your spot in your relationship on equal ground.

You need to find a balance, a fine line between having them accept your terms and being oppressed! You don't want them to feel like you beat them in this game! They must not feel defeated! You just want them to willingly be by your side! Just as they would position themselves for a bigger, stronger, and smarter Female Alpha!

If you can find that balance, you are holding the universe in the palm of your hand! But trust me, you will suffer, go through some trial and error, and fight many battles along the way until you master that skill.

But in general, just like in the animal world, true Alphas of the opposite sex will always be attracted to each other and harmlessly play, changing top positions (no pun intended) as they do, but ultimately, all Alphas gravitate toward the same goal!

So…play around with other Alphas freely but with a sense of caution. Give them space, and enjoy the space that is given to you, but should you engage in a conflict, try to patiently find the root of it, for it might be attraction, and the She Alpha might just be too clumsy in showing affection or not be aware of it herself.

Imaginary Alpha

The ones that you, as an Alpha Male, must really watch for are *Imaginary Alpha Females*!

This creature is in a category all its own! Cold, calculated! She's been hurt and pushed one too many times in life. And for reasons known to her only, and those could be many and God knows how awful, she has declared war on everything and everybody. She's looking out for herself only, and will stop at nothing to get where she's set to go! She rose and became strong and powerful out of fear of ever being hurt again! She developed a thick armor that protects her from the outer world but also blocks out all the light and warmth this world has to offer. Her heart is frozen inside, and she only feels anger and hate. She feels no remorse, love, compassion, or honor! She will walk all over you and anyone else in her path, will resort to unimaginable methods to win, and is *MOST* dangerous when almost defeated or cornered, for that's when she will use all that she possesses in order to turn defeat into victory at the last second! She will stop

OBSERVATION (ENEMIES, FRIENDS, AND EVERYTHING IN BETWEEN)

at *NOTHING*, and nothing is sacred to this creature! I pity them every time I have to slay one, but this IS a matter of survival. If I must destroy one foul creature in order to take another step toward my goal, so be it! I have no regrets. Not everybody can be saved!

Please note that I'm using a figure of speech when I say things such as "slay," "defeat," and so on. This is not meant as a guide to physically or emotionally abusing women.

But make no mistake, sometimes you will have to show some ruthlessness in dealing with certain people. Destroying someone verbally in a debate, or financially by making a business move, or emotionally, sure feels like slaying to them. Unfortunately, sometimes it's necessary.

One fortunate thing about this nemesis is that in almost 100 percent of cases, you will have **NO** problem spotting one from a mile away! They are usually so self-centered and oblivious in their ignorance that hiding their true colors is not even an option for them!

They enjoy being dominant and the center of attention! They feed off the energy that their inferiors release in fear! But your weapon to defeat this monster is relatively simple! And defeating her is what you will need to do because as soon as she recognizes who you are, she'll launch an attack, at first to test your strength and later as an all-out assault to finish you off and make you submissive and obedient! That is what she lives for! It's her soul food! And every time she wins, she becomes bigger and stronger! Her only downfall is that she picked on *YOU!* To show her that she bit off more than she can chew, you need a good game plan! You need to understand her weaknesses, pick her mind gently, find the root of her insecurities, and play that card to your advantage!

Let me tell you about a phenomenon I've noticed over the past few years.

Progressively, the population of men has grown weaker. It's a trend that is continuing. I've also seen a rise in the current female population's strength.

This makes me happy. Strong women who work

on themselves, opt for a higher education, advance in the business world, give it all at the gym, train hard, and demonstrate discipline and dedication.

As good as that may be, it has brought about some who, in that pursuit of strength and success, lost their compass.

This brings me to the subcategory of Imaginary Alpha Females, those women who want to be strong and successful but have lost their grip on any sense of righteousness and common sense. Imaginary Alpha Females confuse strength for rudeness and independence for lack of compassion and empathy.

While being an Imaginary Male Alpha is a chronic condition, the condition of being an Imaginary Alpha Female seems more of an acute nature. Therefore, pointing out their condition to them, calling them on it, or tactically steering them toward recognition of their mistakes may benefit them.

Now that we've covered that list, let's further discuss the contrast between a true Alpha and an Imaginary one. I feel that as an Alpha, I don't have to announce my status or intentionally intimidate others or make them feel inferior. My true strength lies in my self-confidence and awareness. I don't need to put others down to feel taller, and you shouldn't either.

I say, be righteous. Be confident. Be compassionate and understanding. Be honest. First and foremost toward yourself.

Usually, I quote an author or philosopher I really love, and oftentimes, that's enough to make a difference. Here's a particularly powerful quote that comes to mind:

Rudeness is a weak person's imitation of strength.
—Eric Hoffer

This is so true and well said. I think of this quote to

OBSERVATION (ENEMIES, FRIENDS, AND EVERYTHING IN BETWEEN)

remind myself and others of such a fact when needed. It usually strikes home and guides those in question out of their oblivious mindset (me included).

Chances are, once defeated, that person will be reborn and might even adopt our way! As I've said more than once throughout the course of this book, show compassion to everybody! Everyone deserves a second chance! If you can save someone's soul and give them the tools necessary to better themselves and even gain redemption for past deeds, let it be so! This goes for Imaginary Alphas as well.

You grow when those around you grow! Every time you help somebody, you grow with them! It's an unstoppable process! Ask yourself why teachers teach kids around the world even when their wages don't reflect the hard work they put in day in and day out! It's the satisfaction of helping someone learn and grow! They are setting pillars on the foundation of future big minds! Besides parents, teachers are responsible for helping you choose your life path! They can show you the way and give you the tools but can also be your downfall if they do it for the wrong reasons! Here I refer to your parents, for some of them tend to shape their children into a mold they failed to become. So, let yourself be a teacher to others! Let them follow you. Show them the way while letting them find some truths on their own! Allow them to reach a sense of accomplishment as their prize! Inspire them to teach others! That should be your legacy! What you should strive for ultimately! Pass on your knowledge!

Knowledge is our weapon against darkness and primitivism! Our light in the darkness of the night! Our path toward a better tomorrow! Maybe one day, after we have amassed enough followers, who will go on to amass followers of their own, and so on, we can set out on that journey to fight *Ultimate Evil!* Those few who are untouchable now! Sitting in their golden tower pulling strings and making most of us dance as they play! It's a distant dream, naïve even, but not **IMPOSSIBLE!** Maybe one day, the children of our children will live to see it done!

I feel that in introducing the Imaginary Alpha and warning you of such obstacles you may encounter on your journey to New You, I have already touched upon the next topic.

So, let us continue in that same spirit and explore further threats.

CHAPTER 9

DANGERS

Apart from those obvious dangers we all have to watch out for and the threats that might arise from enemies we've just learned to recognize, there are other potential problems you must remain vigilant about!

Becoming an Alpha means growing confident!

Unfortunately, in the process of becoming an Alpha, there's a very real danger of growing *overconfident!*

You'd be surprised at how easy it is to cross that line! And it happens to ALL of us at some point! You will begin to believe in yourself and your abilities so much, you will start to consider yourself untouchable… Unstoppable!

It's like the kind of adrenaline rush that comes with playing and competing in sports! Jump higher, go faster, lift more, cheat death a few more times!

It becomes your obsession to find your limits. To test your strength to the breaking point!

It WILL happen. When it DOES, be careful! You'll find yourself approaching a beautiful woman while she's there with her fiancé—and maybe six of his football teammates.

You'll try to protect the innocent even if it means fighting many and endangering yourself! You will take on so much responsibility at work that it'll eventually crush you! You'll challenge another Alpha when your gut is telling you not to! That is all part of your evolution, and while it's a good thing, you need not get hurt or worse because of it! The answer to this potential dilemma is to learn to choose your battles!

You need not engage in every battle that comes your way! Choose the ones you're sure you can win or at least sure are worth fighting for! Remember one thing! Just like how your credit score is tabulated, every time you engage in a battle, it gets noted, and every defeat will lower your score on the big blackboard of life! So, be wise in choosing when to take action! Don't blindly rush in and throw yourself out there! There's no need to eagerly accept every challenge! Remember, other Alphas have their eye on you, and they, too, choose their battles and plan ahead for them! Ask yourself, *If I do this, will I just become a stepping stone on this Alpha's road to greatness?*

If you smell a trap, back off, regroup, and return to fight another day! Don't necessarily follow some imaginary code and be too proud to step back! Remember my previous message in this book!

SOMETIMES YOU NEED TO TAKE STEP BACK IN ORDER TO MOVE FORWARD!

Another thing to bear in mind: In that euphoric moment after the battle and your subsequent victory, remember your honor—and that golden rule between combatants. There's no honor in victory if you embarrass your opponent! Having said that, by all means, defeat if and when you can, but don't make fools out of those you conquer! As mentioned, often you and the people you face can become best friends, but if you embarrass those you encounter, beating them into the ground and then stomping on them a few times for good measure, chances are, you will create an enemy for life! And if you and I agree on one thing above all else, it's that we **don't** need more of those, *right?*

So, show respect and valor in life and war. Do what

DANGERS

is necessary, but don't dishonor your opponents! Think about how you would feel if you were so dishonored. It would induce Anger...Hate... Thoughts of vengeance! You don't want to find yourself in bed, thinking about how some stupid mistake from your past will come back to haunt you! Trust me. Shake hands with your rival; it'll make both of you better men!

There's another danger you will be prone to, and with this, I can't really help you. I can only relate. Being an Alpha means being a leader, and that, in turn, means being protective, among other things. Now, I have this problem. It is an ongoing issue that I'm working hard to figure out and deal with. Perhaps it just comes with the territory.

My friends like to call me Captain Justice! And I think it comes with my Alpha status! I can't stand injustice! Now, when it's directed to me, that's quite okay. I'm always willing to stand up for myself and fight, and I want you to do the same.

The problem is that I get involved in conflicts that shouldn't concern me! I can't help it! If I see someone in trouble, someone being harassed for no reason, or any other type of injustice directed toward the helpless among us, I step up!

Repeatedly, I have found myself involved in things that, some would argue, shouldn't have concerned me.

I have witnessed cruelty toward animals many times and reacted, rushing to those poor creatures' aid.

I have witnessed domestic abuse and acted in defense of the weak and unprotected party.

I have prevented unfair fights on the street if I felt one side was outnumbered or unjustly attacked, and during my wartime service, protected and saved civilians and hostages alike, doing all I could to ensure that the innocent were taken out of harm's way.

I believe this speaks to my frustration with the world we live in, with everything that is wrong around us. The suffering I'm exposed to every day and the hypocrisy! This society teaches us to be humanitarians to help those in need! You see families on the verge of starvation donating money to charity, as well as those middle-class souls (which, by today's standards, means they barely have enough to get by) helping a homeless or sick child in Africa, donating **$32.00** per month for food and medicine.

Meanwhile, multi-billion-dollar companies that earned their riches upon the backs of those middle-class citizens, don't spend their wealth on the needy. Instead, they host insanely lavish parties that come with price tags far above what the average citizen makes in a lifetime. Spilling bottles of Cristal, eating caviar, promoting ridiculous things on which they can waste even more hard-milked money! Consider how much governments are spending on defense systems to protect us from… *WHAT?* Aliens? Themselves?

Why not use all that money to do good in this world?! Why only host charity events when it's for a tax break and good PR? Why do those who have the most spend the least on worthwhile causes? Where is the balance? Is that how we want to live?

THAT'S why I stand by everyone who is oppressed. Who wants to make a difference, to help! And I know I should! Everything inside me is telling me to do it! On the other hand, it's counterproductive to what I've set out to be! It holds me back sometimes! I get in trouble over things I can't control! That's why I need to teach myself to stop! Not to turn my head away, just to try to help on a different level! To look at the big picture!

I need to find a way to distance myself from those things, to keep striving toward my goal and then, when I reach my rightful place in society's ladder, to do something good from that position! Use the power I have, the knowledge I've armed myself with, and hopefully, the wealth I've gathered along the way to make a difference! Do something that **REALLY** counts to help those in need.

Lead by example, and make a huge deal out of it when you do! Show others—the ones with wealth in particular—that it's okay to give and share…. It's okay to be **HUMAN**, to

DANGERS

think of others for a change! Unfortunately, this can bring about its own set of issues. It can put eyes on you, push you into the spotlight—where it's not always safe to be. By pushing for change, you start making ripples, disturbing that calm surface! And the bigger of a rock you become, the bigger the ripples you create! Think about it. If you can get other rocks to throw themselves into the water, heralding big changes in the world, it will create a major disturbance! And many won't like that much and will do everything in their power to prevent it.

This has been the kind of journey I've undertaken, and it's come with its share of pitfalls. I mention all this to help you make your own decisions based on what I've encountered! More than anything, I want you to exercise caution. It's not always wise to leap into the fray, even for the greater good. It's like trying to take on a three-headed hydra. More heads tend to form when you chop off one or two. So, as you work on growing into your best you, don't grow overconfident or try to take on too much. Be smart, be cautious, and always remember the consequences!

Next, I would like to warn you and teach you a few useful tactics.

Avoid falling for a trap of over-promoting yourself.

There will be times when NOT showing your full potential will be critical to your success! Yes, often you must give 110 percent to get what you want, but you will find circumstances in which you'll have to downgrade a notch or two to prosper! At work, with your boss, for example. People in charge like intelligent and fast-learning team members, but show too much initiative and brains, and you will find yourself outside the magic circle with little or no chance of coming back. So, yes, I suggest that you trick them. Let them think you are just smart enough for them to use you and your ideas and knowledge to their advantage and climb the ladder over your back. They won't mind if you take their place once they are gone, but not before! *NEVER* before! So just lay low and wait for your opportunity. Don't worry whether you are smarter, more resourceful, or more charismatic than your superior! Show initiative where and when it counts, and soon, you won't be taking his position but jumping over his to the next spot in the corporate ladder that your superior had his eye on for so long! Again, do not make him or her look bad in the process! Just prove to be the better and more suited candidate for the responsibilities that position demands!

So, to sum it up, never present yourself as a threat to your superior! That mistake will result in you starting again from the bottom elsewhere! Play your cards right, and advancement will be inevitable! Listen to what your gut is telling you!

I know it sounds like I'm asking much of you.

We've covered a lot of goals and potential missteps, such as looking out for enemies, educating yourself, bringing your body into a superb physical state, practicing social skills, and avoiding overconfidence!

But that will just be a day in the office for you once you evolve into who you need to be! Much of what I've covered so far will come naturally once you realize your full potential. Education brings work prosperity.

An appealing and healthy physical appearance brings more social confidence and attention from the opposite sex.

Language and humor make for a charming personality. Playing an instrument will make you popular with those around you as well as give you pleasure of accomplishment and a fun past time activity!

Learn how to play golf even if you hate it! Your boss is sure to like you more! Go fishing with your boss and business partners! Personal and business secrets are often discussed on such outings, when the guys relax among friends! Fishing skills will come in handy with your children!

Learn about food and wine! Women find it sexy when a man knows his way around a kitchen. You might save the day for your boss by choosing the right wine for the occasion! Discreetly make sure that his boss gets a hint that it was, in fact, you who picked up that bottle of Chateau Latour

DANGERS

Pauillac 1990 for his new business partner's birthday party!

Being noticed by the right people at the right time is the key to success! And keep in mind, you are not doing anything wrong here! Nature has always intended the fastest, strongest, intelligent, and wisest to advance. So really, you are just following nature's laws. If your boss was the more competent choice for that position, he would have claimed it for himself long ago! You haven't tricked anyone into believing you were the best; you've just made them realize it! That's all! That's nothing to be ashamed of. You've used the tools given to you by nature to advance in the natural order! Though we now live in a jungle made of steel, concrete, wood, and plastic, it is still only a *JUNGLE!* And jungle rules still apply! Play by them to your advantage, and you'll have the formula for success!

There are many more dangers—too many to list them all here, in fact. We are all individuals. Our paths will differ slightly, so I can't warn you about everything that is out there, but what I've been happy to do is provide some general rules to live by. Follow them, never let your guard down, trust your instincts and judgment, and you will be just fine! I'm not worried about you, and you shouldn't be either! Trust yourself because you are the only true ally you have! If you ever find yourself in a corner, with no plan and your defenses down, do not despair! Remember my advice: Back off, cut your losses, and move on, wiser for that experience! Learn from it so that you're never caught off guard again!

It matters not who wins one battle or three... What matters is who wins the war! And this war is lifelong, so prepare yourself to lose a battle or two! It's all part of the growth process! Part of that circle of nature! What doesn't kill us makes us stronger, so take it with you and be better for it! If you learn something from a mistake, call it a lesson, not a defeat.

Be on alert always and play your cards smart! Don't bluff too much, though! It won't pay off in the long run! It's always better to win using your advantages and with your heart!

OMEGA TO ALPHA

That's my advice to you!

So far, I've talked a lot about the work you need to put in, the effort and discipline.

I don't think I've fully addressed one very important aspect of your journey, however.

And that is to embrace and enjoy the process.

---

*On the way to the top, don't forget
to stop and enjoy the view!*

—Dejan Garalejic

The key to having the best experience possible as you grow into an Alpha is simple.

BALANCE.

CHAPTER 10

BALANCE

I know. I've made everything I've listed in this book seem SO important that you must immediately make it your top priority.

Like you should channel all your time and energy toward that ultimate goal.

And you should!

Just not *ALL* the time!

You must find balance in everything you do, or you will lose your focus and desire to succeed! You have to learn to pace yourself; set small, realistic, short-term goals; and follow those to the top and ultimate prize.

Setting smaller and more readily achievable objectives will ensure that your motivation stays high and will also give you satisfaction.

Getting your hair cut to better complement your appearance is a good example, as is losing a few pounds, getting a teeth cleaning, or fitting into a new suit.

Learn a few new words and how to incorporate them into your everyday vocabulary.

Win that girl's attention and set a date with her.

Anything that will give you a sense of accomplishment in a short time.

By achieving those, you'll get a sense of accomplishment and satisfaction and feed your inner fire, which will only make you hungrier and ready to take on new, bigger obstacles on your way! Once you can manage the small details, the big picture will come together effortlessly! It's true!

Words to live by!

Great acts are made up of small deeds.

—Lao Tzu

Let's take a moment to reflect on a very old story and what it can teach us.

One day, I happened upon a story written by Sean O'Connor called, "Socrates On Wisdom." I think it really speaks to the main thrust of my message.

At first, the wisdom contained within this story seemed so powerful, I believed such a philosophy should be adopted by all, at all costs, but after giving it much thought, I decided that I didn't agree with that idea.

Let's look at the story first, and then I'll break down my view of it.

One day a proud young man approached Socrates and asked him to show him the path to wisdom. Socrates looked at the man and paused for a few moments, allowing him to become uncomfortable with the silence. He locked eyes with the young man and told him, "meet me at the river at dawn" before walking away.

The next morning the young man arrived at the river before dawn. Socrates soon walked down the path and slowly waded into the water, motioning for the man to join him. When the young man waded up to his chest Socrates looked at him and asked, "what do you want?" The young man responded, "to find wisdom!"

Socrates grabbed the man and began drowning him. He held him under water for twenty seconds and then let him up, asking him again, "what do you want?" The young man responded again, "to find wisdom!" At that, Socrates promptly submerged the man under water again. Thirty seconds passed, then forty, and the man's face began to turn blue. Socrates lifted the man up and asked, "what do you want?" The man gasped, "air!"

Socrates released the young man, and said "when you want wisdom as much as you have just wanted air, then you will begin to find wisdom."

You can find the full story on Medium.com at: https://medium.com/@aseoconnor/socrates-on-wisdom-28057a0951.

First off...I'm fully aware that I'm not nearly intelligent or educated enough to challenge Socrates! I'm just smart enough to know I shouldn't even try!

In fact, I do agree with his teaching. It's us, people in general, who are in the wrong. We often misinterpret the wisdom of others. Many will translate this great story into something that it's not. It's been used mostly in circles that teach us about business and material success! And that, to me, is completely wrong! I'm not going to question the teaching methods of others or somebody's desires. All I'm saying here is that we, too, should apply this story and let it guide us on our journey!

But think about it. Most people interpret this wonderful example as nothing but a metaphor for gaining business success and winning that quest for wealth!

That is the furthest we can go from what I'm trying to teach you here!

Yes, you should want it badly enough to become the best!

Only, you need to want to be the best at everything! What lies behind most people who are wealthy and successful in business?! Broken marriages, unhappy children, cheating, lawyers, divorces, illness! They want that power and success so badly, just like that boy wanted air, that they neglect all other aspects of their life! They get so consumed by that chase that it becomes the only thing they care about! Ambition is like a black hole that keeps growing and growing, eventually swallowing everything in its way and consuming its creator! And the reason for that is simple: Human greed is limitless! And if we let it control us, we are lost! It has driven many before us to madness and hell!

---

*He who knows that enough is enough
will always have enough.*

—Lao Tzu

Don't make the mistake of wanting too much!
Sometimes we get so wrapped up in ambition, often driven by the suggestions of others, that we forget OUR goals. That's why it's so crucial to keep a journal in which you can often reflect on and check your progress.
Not everyone has the same ambition. Some desire power. Others want business success. For others, success is just a means to an end; they may wish to help others and utilize their financial success for this purpose.
Lao Tzu teaches us not to get lost in greed and ambition. Know exactly what you want. Think long and hard before you decide what will make you happy.
There's a quote I love by well-known Serbian author Dusan Radovic:
"Before you set out on a journey to find happiness, stop and think about your life. For it could be that you're ALREADY happy, but just don't know it. For happiness is sometimes small and hard to notice, and many fail to recognize it."
Live by Socrates's words, but apply them to all aspects of your life! Desire that success, strive to reach stardom, think big and wide! Just don't do it only to gain power or wealth!

BALANCE

Be the best you can be.
The best husband…
Best father…
Best driver…
Best at whatever it is you do…
Look your best, and don't get outspoken!

Learn and master as many new skills as you can but not at the expense of losing other important things in your life. You can't be truly successful until you've experienced true love, true friendship, the birth of a child, the loss of someone dear to your heart! There are so many experiences out there that make life what it is! You need to participate in all of them, good and bad, because they define who you are and who you will become! How would we know the meaning of true happiness if we never experienced a true sorrow, and vice versa? How can we value life if we've never created one?! How can we define a true friend if we've never had one by our side?! Because, at the end of the day, when everything is said and done, when you sit in your rightfully deserved (metaphorical) throne, looking back at your past life, proud of who you became and what you've done, remember one thing: Success is meaningless without people to share it with! A new material thing might seem shiny, but you can't take it with you when you go. And whatever your shiny new material thing might be, you're bound to get bored with it very fast! The same goes for experiences we partake in alone. Thrills we may have loved once inevitably become dull, leading to new ways to find that rush, which, in turn, leads to problems and more despair. A lot of successful people develop addictions! Alcohol, drugs, sex, gambling… any of which will hammer the last few nails in the coffin of your happiness and past life, and you'll find yourself living hell on Earth!

Remember two things.
It's lonely at the top if you bring no one with you.
And my favorite saying:

OMEGA TO ALPHA

The best things in life aren't things!
—Art Buchwald

Keep that in mind *ALWAYS*. Ask yourself daily why you are doing this. Keep your goals clear and in mind! Write them down and keep them safe.

Take it one day at a time, and keep working on those small goals and details. Perfect that little puzzle piece before you fit it onto that big board. I know the picture can seem enormous, and sometimes you'll lose sight of it. That's how overwhelming it can be, but as long as we have those little pieces, and they lock into all the previous ones, we are on the right track.

If we are facing the right direction, all we have to do is keep walking.
—Buddhist proverb

Visualize your path and goal and keep walking. There's no point running because you never know when you might arrive. We're far more successful making slow, calculated steps than running carelessly!

So, to sum it up, finding the perfect balance is hard. It's a constant process, and it's not easy, but no one told you this was going to be a walk in the park! I would never promise you that! But if you're constantly juggling and keeping that balance in check, the benefits will be many and can't be measured by numbers or statistics! Having happy family and friends around you, having people who follow you and trust you, being able to sleep at night with a clear conscience, and making others happy and satisfied will show you the true meaning of being successful! Everything you ever did and every sacrifice you made to get to that point will suddenly

BALANCE

make perfect sense and inspire you to do more! That is the greatest achievement in anybody's lifetime! To leave a positive mark on others!

CHAPTER 11

PERSONAL EXPERIENCE

At the beginning, I made a decision not to talk too much about myself in this book. Partially due to the fact that I want to keep my privacy and confidentiality, and in part because I strongly believe this book is a self-help tool and, as such, should be *ALL* about *YOU!* After giving it much thought, I decided that stating a few facts and sharing several experiences might be helpful and validate what I'm teaching here!

So, as previously mentioned, I lost my father at an early age. My brother suffered the greater misfortune of never consciously meeting him. At the fragile age of seven, I was faced with enormous responsibility! Unknowingly at the time, I took on a burden I was too young and unprepared to carry, and time would prove just how gigantic a struggle it would be to stay on the path I'd chosen. My dad's shoes were just too large to fill. I remember trying and failing, in my eyes anyway, to recreate my father for my mom and younger brother! Throughout all my trial and error, I also learned, most of the time the hard way, what I could and could not do! As I matured, I realized I didn't have to try so hard to resemble him. Instead, I could resemble what he represented! I didn't have to make jokes the way he used to and make us all laugh ourselves to tears. I could tell my own jokes and trigger the same reaction.

In other words, I didn't have to do things *HIS* way. I just had to act like somebody who had responsibility for my family. Be the head of the house, if you will.

That very day, I kicked his shoes off as far as I could, where I could never find them again, put on my brand-new shiny shoes, and started to cut my own path for me and my family the best I knew how!

My mother recognized the efforts I was putting toward my growth and encouraged me at every opportunity! She was always my best friend and mentor, but instead of teaching me what she knew, she often let me reach my own conclusions. She believed in me and raised me with a sense of responsibility and accomplishment! It was a lot to deal with. Like I didn't have enough on my plate already with puberty, teen years, school, and chores.

Yet I took on this challenge with everything I had and swore (to myself) to meet it to the best of my abilities! My childhood was an ordinary one, but the parallel path I was taking, accepting responsibility for my pack, absorbed so much of me and my energy! I never did all that great in school! Not because I wasn't intelligent enough—quite the opposite, in fact! I used my intelligence to deploy the least amount of work needed to get satisfying results! My battle with school was an easy win for me... On the other front, however, things weren't going so smoothly! I lost much of my childhood with my father's premature departure. I had to grow up in a hurry and skip those careless years of childhood, normally filled with no worries or responsibilities. But I was also born stubborn! I had a drive that kept me going through life! Optimism was planted deep in my being! I kept a sense of humor, a bright spirit, and an open mind and always spoke the truth and my mind, even when I was not asked for my opinion! Believe me, that got me into more trouble than I

PERSONAL EXPERIENCE

care to remember! I liked to battle my fights alone, only telling others about them after the fact. Win or lose, it didn't matter! I was watching my brother grow up, and I wanted to somehow lay the foundation for him to be the kind of man our dad was and that I was so eagerly striving to be!

I remember my dad well. He was a tall man and handsome in his early years. With time, as happens to us all, he became less eye-pleasing! But he had a strong personality and held himself high. He left an impression everywhere he went and spoke with brevity, getting to the point fast, with a strong voice—and people paid attention when he did! He was the CEO of a big export/import corporation, responsible for managing many people and tasks there. I will always remember his air of authority! He was respected and always carried himself with confidence and pride.

Naturally, I wanted to become like him someday. I started noticing human behavior—emotional patterns and reactions, first in movies, books, and comics, and then in real life. I unconsciously learned how to recognize Alphas and strived to act like them. All those characters I admired in real life or fiction were strong, both physically and mentally, had confidence, and were just, but at the same time were educated, well- and soft-spoken, and displayed an emotional side they weren't afraid to show in public. I wanted to be that guy one day! To do great things in life! To have my future child want to follow in my footsteps!

So, I observed and learned, ultimately graduating from the school of life with far better grades than the brick-and-mortar school I attended. I have NO regrets over how I sacrificed my education at that point for life knowledge! I loved to read and educated myself a little bit about everything. Then I expanded that knowledge, subject by subject, until I became known as the GO-TO guy when information was needed. To this day, I store a pretty unbelievable amount of information in my head and am extremely versatile in all the subjects I discuss. I've always challenged myself, engaging in verbal debates, teaching myself things I knew nothing about. I've learned from every argument I took part in, every book or article I read, and every movie and play I ever saw.

I only wish I had the internet at my disposal back then. I could have absorbed so much more information, and far more easily.

I take pride in my verbal skills. I'm still working *EVERY* day on my vocabulary and trying to learn terms and definitions that I'm not so familiar with!

To continue my life retrospective, as we grew and developed, I noticed my brother was becoming like me in many ways. My confidence and courage rubbed off on him; I could see his personality and path becoming more defined.

Unfortunately, Father's death wasn't our greatest setback.

Mother became almost terminally ill after a surgical procedure. We had some family issues and problems that resulted in physical and mental abuse by two family members who I will not name, but I still feel it should be mentioned. My brother and I experienced constant mental torture and sometimes light physical punishment for things we didn't do at the hands of these family members. It was incredibly painful and felt like an attempt to break my brother's and my spirits. I strongly believe that if I had been an ordinary child, if I hadn't taken on my transformation earlier, it would have broken me and locked down that Alpha in me, making it a slave to the Omega who would have commanded the majority of my personality. But since I wasn't *THAT* guy, I strongly rebelled against that oppression. I looked them in the eyes as they continued their emotional abuse, and I knew at that moment, though they might have been winning the moment, I won the war! They couldn't break me! I was stronger than them, beyond their reach! Their cruel words bounced off the wall of confidence I had erected, their actions fading in their impact until any effect they might have had stopped altogether!

WE WON!

The three of us held together, withstanding many storms while always knowing more was coming our way!

WE WERE READY!

PERSONAL EXPERIENCE

For a while, our lives remained peaceful and calm. I continued to improve, to discover new things I could do with my knowledge and strength. I signed up for martial arts classes and attended gym frequently, working on my physical abilities! Somewhere along the way, I discovered the opposite sex and the charms girls carried. I practiced my skills and wit every chance I got. When I reflect on those times, I realize how much I enjoyed my journey, which led me to become who I am today. I urge you to take that step, to close your eyes and believe. Let my words and your senses guide you, and take that leap of faith! You WILL have a blast along your journey! I promise you that!

Years went by, and I became a young man! Always the one to organize events, parties, camping trips, etcetera! The one with the good ideas, willing to try and explore new things! I gained many friends and acquaintances. I was, and still am, loved among those who know me. I am blessed to have met so many wonderful souls on my journey, many of whom I still call close friends. I always kept my family together.

Then, out of nowhere, war came upon us. I went in for my military service, which, where I come from, is mandatory for a year. I'm not going to go into details and talk about the military or the horrors of war, the pain and suffering I saw from so many, the unnecessary loss of life, the hundreds of thousands left homeless on all three sides, or the nightmare of an uncertain future left for those who spent over a decade trapped in constant fighting and danger. I've seen things that I wish I never did. I lost people I wish I could bring back. We all did. War touched *EVERY SINGLE* soul and family, and it's something I wouldn't wish upon anybody, anywhere, anytime. The army toughened me up, gave me the skills and training to take care of myself in any situation. As terrible as the war was, it gave me even more strength and formed a thick crust around my soul, hardening that shell we all have to protect ourselves from the outside world. But most importantly, war taught me to value life...*THE MOST!*

I learned how fragile life was and how easy it can

diminish. During that time, I learned about taking life as well as sparing it. There are two ways of giving life on this earth; both are equally highly spiritual experiences. There's the miracle of birth, more for females but also very much for us guys. And there's that moment when you save or spare someone's life. In that moment, you learn about yourself and others. You get so close to the center of your being, and believe me when I say this... So does the other person!

In all that horror and destruction, I took lessons with me, which I'll hold onto for as long as I live.

Only the dead have seen the end of war.
— Plato

It's true! Others are cursed to carry the horror of war and destruction deep in their souls, as a reminder of who we can become if we can't gain full control over who we truly are! And it's a good thing for most of those involved! As I said, it's impossible to appreciate what's good if you never experience anything bad. I now know and value who I am because I know what I could've been and what that side of me is capable of.

I want to stop here and reflect on something. I'm sure that you all will experience something similar at some point, at least to a certain degree. We can't all have the same experiences, but we all go through rough patches in our lives. We have all struggled and been hurt. We've fought battles and lost them. We've lost loved ones along the way. Some of us have even lost ourselves. But in the end, we survived. Every struggle made us stronger. Every mistake, wiser. Every person we lost taught us about the fragility and value of life.

Don't be ashamed of the scars from your life battles. Wear them proudly as medals of honor. As a testament to your personal growth.

Wear them as your armor, your defense against future attacks.

PERSONAL EXPERIENCE

It means you survived, that you're still here, and still have fight and strength in you.

Okay, let's switch gears to something that feels as far from war and strife as possible but is equally important. Let's talk about love.

It could be love for a spouse, friend, child, or country. Whatever your motives are, love makes you stronger! It's the single most important feeling in this universe that defies all laws of nature! There's no scientific explanation for what love truly is or does, but it inspires us to be better, faster, more creative! We become capable of the unimaginable, surpass limits never known to man before, break all the rules and boundaries. We break free!

Being deeply loved by someone gives you strength, while loving someone deeply gives you courage.

—Lao Tzu

Just be careful; love is a *POWERFUL* tool. As much creativity as it carries, it brings even more destruction! But if you can manage to keep all your affairs in order, love should serve as a tool for achieving that ultimate state talked about in this book that we are all after.

Love is a crucial ingredient for balance! Remember that!

In Serbia, after the war, we faced an enormous economic crisis and other life problems. But all that seemed insignificant and small compared to what I had gained!

A new accomplice. A new member of my pack!

I found my She Alpha!

She changed my life forever and made it better, not only filling it with love, happiness, and joy but also new strength, support, and energy.

She was the pillar that, in conjunction with my foundation, would support our life together. She took over half the burden and carried it proudly. We worked as a team.

Stronger together than the sum of our parts, she stood by my side proudly. I knew that everything we set out to achieve would be easier to attain. "Team" replaced "Me," and I was okay with that.

She gave me two of my most valuable possessions: our little angels!

When my son was born, everything became clear. My life's purpose, my struggles, all the pain and suffering suddenly held meaning! I saw my path clearly and **FAR** into the future. Everything I'd ever learned poured into that one moment. The universe stopped for some time, and I recognized my purpose. Everything I ever did in life, every little thing, even the silliest step I ever took, led me to this point!

Now I was responsible for a much bigger pack! For a small and helpless member of it! That became my mission. All eyes were fixed on me, and I needed to shine brighter than ever.

But I was no longer alone in this.

I said earlier that your Female half is your ultimate prize! And she **IS!** She will be the reason you wake up in the morning, work so hard, and go to bed at night. She truly will be your better half! She is wise, calculated, and holds all the strings that will make all your family members function as a pack! She will let you lead as she follows and support you to the death, if it comes to that, but she will also be the voice of reason.

She is the one who will bring *FINAL* balance into your life!

She completes the circle. Everything else is just fine-tuning. Little adjustments!

She holds the key!

And you should never fail to show her that. Never shy away from your feelings. The stereotypical "macho man" is the wrong perception of an Alpha Male!

I hope you've sufficiently learned this in my book. That machismo is fake and, as a concept, should be obliterated!

Celebrate your love and show your feelings.

Take care of her as she does you. Make her feel loved and appreciated. Make her happy.

PERSONAL EXPERIENCE

Love is not about taking, it's truly all about giving, and the more you give, the more you will have.

Remember that life is all about little things. Little signs of affection. Little things that you do to make other people feel loved and needed.

Use EVERY opportunity to show your Female Alpha that she's special to you and appreciated.

In my opinion, this is where we differ most from all other animal examples. As an Alpha, you should find, keep, and cherish that one loyal life partner whom you chose. If you're lucky enough for her to choose you as well!

It'll make you a better man, and that is what this book is all about!

Believe me, your She Alpha will appreciate that, and you will be rewarded generously!

As for the little ones...

Well, train them from a young age.

Make sure they feel loved and needed. Praise them a lot. Show them they are better. Show them the path and let them follow. That's an advantage they will have over you! They are born with that Alpha potential and they have you to guide them. Just keep them on that trail. I'll let you write your own chapters here... You will want to!

To sum up this chapter, our life path eventually led us to relocate to Canada, and with that, we took that giant step toward a new beginning. Never be shy of starting over! It puts a new, fresh perspective on your life! Imagine if you took a wrong turn and got stuck wandering hopelessly, getting more and more lost until no hope remained of ever finding the right track.

Now imagine if you could reset and start from the beginning! Wouldn't you want to?

So, why is it so hard and scary starting life over, making big changes and moves? You are still you! You're just taking a different, better course! And you've learned from past mistakes and experiences. You get a clean slate, even if this one is five thousand miles away from the old slate. You still know what to do and how to do it! So, roll up your sleeves and get to work!

And we did! We worked LONG and HARD, and we are proud of it. Now, in Canada, I have more possibilities, more opportunities to expand my knowledge, to better myself.

Plus, I have several big advantages over people who've lived here all their lives.

First of all, I'm an Alpha! Second, I know how hard life can be. I know what hunger, pain, and suffering is. I know how to appreciate opportunities in this wonderful land as they come my way and how to take advantage of them! This society made you who you are. But I see differently because I came as an outsider, and I can help you. I can wake you up, shake you out of that lethargy. I can show you the way and give you the tools to break free from this hell. I want to pull you out of that hamster wheel and have you think for yourself for once! To realize you are worth it! You are destined for greatness, but you need to see that for yourself! So, wake up from this society-induced coma you spent your past life in! Open your mind; let go of everything holding you back! Grab my hand and hear my voice, and together, we can show the world who you really are!

But you need to want it!

You need to fight for it! To see that Matrix yourself!

Just like in the movie *The Matrix*, once you acknowledge and familiarize yourself with it and its rules, you'll be able to take advantage of it and make it work **FOR** you, not against you. And the more trapped people you free, the better you'll feel! You'll draw power from their energy and become a better and stronger version of yourself! **YES**, I'm doing this for you, but I'm also doing it for me! Let us delve deeper into why I'm comparing current society to a Matrix-type framework. I'll show you what's going on, what the rules are, how to move forward, and together, we can rule this life!

CHAPTER 12

THE MATRIX

It seems to me that today's society could be defined as The Matrix.

I want to apologize for the lack of a better term, but I'm not sure what else to call it. For those who have seen the movie, you will agree it's the perfect synonym, while those who haven't probably think I've finally lost it.

If you are familiar with the movie or at least the term and its meaning, skip to the next chapter. If you don't, read on.

The movie *The Matrix* features an artificial reality of the same name. The Matrix is comprised of a gigantic system of machines that hold pods, created for enslaved humans to live in. All humanity is kept in this hive-like environment, and the machines use the electrochemical charge our bodies create to power their entire artificial world!

In simple language, they've turned humans into living batteries to harvest until their death. To keep us complacent in our pods, they created the Matrix, an artificial reality in which we all believe we are alive and well, that we live our lives and have dreams and hopes and jobs. So, while we were falling in love, arguing with our spouse, acing those last school exams, enjoying our first kiss, winning the lottery, or so many other things, we all actually exist in an artificially induced coma, tricked by a live feed sent directly into our brains that make us believe what we were experiencing. Our brains, being the organ responsible for interpreting our senses, can't tell the difference. Only those who are freed in the movie by those who've managed to find their way back to reality can awaken and face the frightening truth: that the world is cruel, cold, full of danger, and ugly!

After I watched the movie, I recalled asking myself:

Why would anyone want to wake up from that dream? Why give up all the security and future offered by The Matrix and choose a life of exile, struggle, and war? Why not just let it go and enjoy the rest of your Matrix life?

The answer was obvious! Because it was an illusion! A construct designed and forced upon you by something else! It doesn't matter how good your life is, if you are not your own man, it's not a real life at all! Who cares about money, fame, or power if you can't make your own decisions and plan your future? Even a gilded cage is still a cage!

You see what I'm getting at. In the movie, a small, courageous crew battle The Matrix and what it represents! They wanted to free the human race! But many didn't want to be saved! Many chose the illusion over facing the responsibilities of real life! And I can understand that! Those were Omegas. But this book is about Alphas.

So, that leads me to ask:

What would you choose?

EXACTLY!

That brings us to here...to now. Where you are, this minute. Why not do it now? In this moment. In this life? Break free from the illusion.

This society is—and let's face facts here—just the same as the one in *The Matrix*, if not worse.

Think about. Rules, boundaries, and parameters you need to follow. Work in a cubicle all your life. One week of vacation time, no sick days. Keep your head down. Don't

THE MATRIX

speed when you drive. Opt for an economy model because it saves on gas, spares the environment, and is cheaper on the insurance. Get your ID and carry it with you always. Speak respectfully to authority figures even when you know they are wrong. The teacher is always right, even when you know you know better. Same with your boss. Do your work. Punch in, punch out. Eat when society gives you a lunch break. Pay taxes. Get a loan and/or credit card. Use it because it improves your credit score. Pay your bills on time to avoid penalties. Brush your teeth with this toothpaste because four out of five dentists recommend it. Remember: The legal blood alcohol level is 0.08 percent. Don't disturb the peace by making too much noise. If you are too happy, you most likely have ADHD. If you are too calm, you most likely suffer from depression. Go to your doctor; he'll get you on medication in either case! Don't stand out. Wear a school uniform. Don't have too many kids; the world is getting overpopulated! Halloween is on this day; everybody dresses up. If you wait in line, be quiet. Turn your cell phone off and stand on the yellow line. If somebody is hurt, don't try to help them. You might get sued.

But if you have training, you'll get sued if you don't help. If you see injustice toward an individual, turn your back. You might get arrested otherwise. If you have progressive ideas, keep them to yourself. Are we still living in the dark ages?

Is that freedom of speech? Democracy? Is this what so many died fighting for?

They even changed the school system to produce less intelligent and less capable people. Again, please don't get offended, but if you do some research, you will see that schools in Europe, Asia, and even the Middle East are so much more advanced! In my home country, kids learn in the third grade what North American eighth-grade graduates struggle with. That is why educated personnel from foreign countries are far more valued by employers here than locals. Electrical engineers, scientists, and medical experts from all over the world are paid top dollar to come to North America and participate in projects. Meanwhile, you put your child through school, pay hundreds of thousands of dollars toward their education, and what do you get?

YOU, DEAR READER, ARE IN THE MATRIX!

I could go on forever, but I think you get the point! You were molded since birth. Throughout your life, you've worn that mold like a curse! You know deep inside it's wrong and you deserve better, but everybody else seems to get with the program, so better not make waves. The last guy who disturbed the surface ended up in jail or a mental institution. You're a zombie, a machine, programmed to do the same thing over and over until you die. Just think about it!

It's THE MATRIX! Right here and now! And it's scary, perfected, and run by people who know their job well.

As I mentioned, beating that beast is almost impossible and unrealistic as a goal, but breaking out of this prison is possible and depends upon one person only! *YOU!*

First, you need to realize it, understand it, then devise a plan of action and execute it! It will be worse than battling an addiction because you must go against everything you feel is right. But take heart—it will only seem that way. Just because somebody has been telling you your whole life that something is wrong doesn't mean it really is! You have to make your own decisions regarding those choices. Break out of your routine. Do something fresh, set new goals, and make new resolutions.

Always keep in mind that they want you to fail! To place yourself back in the big picture like a good and obedient puzzle piece that slid out before falling back in place! Keep in mind, that they WILL sabotage you! The system is designed that way! There are protective measures against rebels. Built-in firewalls and traps for those who dare to challenge the system. To them, you will be a virus and will get noticed.

Develop a cover in that system. Make it seem like you are going with the flow most of the time. Just choose the paths that work to your advantage! By doing so, eventually, they will lose interest, and you will get more freedom to

THE MATRIX

work on yourself. Remember that they don't want Alphas to exist. We are a threat to the system. We are those who will eventually take over. One by one, as human conscience awakens, we will prevail. They've managed to detain nature's laws, establishing themselves so high and deep that no single Alpha can do anything to challenge them for that top-dog position. And as long as they keep us at bay and control the number of opposition, they are safe!

I know I sound like I should be writing a sci-fi novel, but if you think about it, I probably haven't said anything you already didn't know or suspected.

I'm just stating the obvious, and I ask you to act for your own sake!

Now, if you want to choose to remain part of that Global Scale Scam, be my guest. You bought my book, and that's the only thing that should matter to me, right?

But it's not. Quite the opposite is the case.

I actually care about you!

I want you to become who you can be! To see more people truly happy and successful!

CHAPTER 13

WHOLE PACKAGE

They say that it's lonely at the top. That is partially true.

Being top dog means you will have the attention, respect, and fear of others, but many who notice you will also be potential challengers. There will also be those who lie to your face while enviously plotting behind your back. For those, I say "Let them talk behind you. That means you're still ahead of them!"

Here's the point: You will make many acquaintances as you move along your journey but very few real friends. And that's okay. I don't have many REAL friends, but those who are know that I would die for them, and I know they would do likewise for me.

You will also amass an army of loyal followers over time. These people are very important too. But I will address that topic in a later chapter.

Let's get back to the REAL subject of this book. Let us remind ourselves why we are reading this book and striving to become our true Alphas selves.

By this point, I assume, you've already decided to go

through with this. Why else would you still be reading?! If you are still just playing with this Alpha idea while hoping for some kind of formula or pill at the end of this book to magically transform you into the New You we've been talking about, if you feel there's a shortcut you can take or have somebody else do it for you, you are in denial. You need to rethink this and your life long and hard.

I know the tunnel I'm leading you through is long and dark. It's easy to get lost, and there's no guarantee you'll ever reach its end. But isn't it better to die trying than sit at the entrance until your number is up? To spend an eternity wondering how it would have ended if you'd pulled yourself together and found the courage to take that first step?

I will always choose regret over something I did over something I didn't dare do only to realize later that I should have.

All I'm offering is that light at the end of it... And I'm giving you a way to reach it. And that's more than you'll find traveling through many of the other tunnels you'll end up in during your life. Many of those are dead ends. Many never make it out alive. It's like a maze, really long, dark, and cold. A place easy to get lost in, and all you can hear are the screams and moans of those still lost and wandering. Our tunnel has its ups and downs. You'll stumble over many obstacles and traps, not to mention all the walls that will be put up to block your path. You'll have to go around, leap across, or simply knock them down using your ever-growing strength!

But always keep in mind the reason why we are doing this!

Stay focused!

Never let that slip away! Seek that light, and once you find it, keep it in sight. Move toward it with everything you've got. Every person's journey is unique and individual; there's no time frame I can set for any of you to reach it. There's no late or early *in* reaching that inner balance. It will just come to you one day, not a second too soon or too late. And you will know! Nobody can describe to you how that feels. But you will know when it happens because you've been destined for that since birth. And long before. It's in your genes. Nature intended us to be all we could be; many of us have simply forgotten that. We've been altered. Outside factors now dictate to us to think and feel differently. Generation after generation, we lose further touch with nature. Our senses have grown dull.

Think about it.

Dogs are beloved, domesticated companions. Long before they became that way, dogs were wolves who ran wild in nature. Wolves only became dogs after a long domestication process, during which these animals learned to enjoy the safety and comfort that living by man's side offered.

The first dogs to appear were Omega wolves. They eschewed their loyalty to their original pack and Alpha leader to enter human habitats to offer obedience and submission in exchange for protection from a new leader and pack.

Dogs grew more adjusted to life alongside man and adopted different behaviors over time.

Dog became man's best friend. But is he really our friend? Are we not his Alpha pack leader?

Their ancient genetics are still strong, and not all dogs are born submissive. At an early age, this manifests the most. That's why it's necessary to "train" your dog during the early days of your relationship. We basically turn them into Omegas and assert our will and dominance to control them and ensure their obedience.

If you listen to dog trainers, you will notice how they emphasize the need to show your dog who is the pack leader of the family. Once a dog recognizes his/her place in the family hierarchy, only then does it become an obedient and good pet. All we do, really, is teach the dog that we are its leader. We are the Alpha, the one it must heed and obey. As long as your dog knows you are the pack's Alpha, it will be calm and won't bark or attack other dogs or strangers. It will let YOU take charge of that duty. That's why in some families, dogs act completely different when the man of the house is not around. If others try to walk it or give commands, it will come across as rebellious and try imposing its will. Often dogs don't listen to kids or females. In extreme cases, when you treat your pet as equal and let him/her do whatever they please, you will encounter a situation where a dog might even try to bite you. That's because you didn't set the boundaries and rules, and the dog is testing its limits! *EVERY SINGLE OPPORTUNITY IT GETS!*

So…is a dog really our friend? You either have an obedient dog that learns rules and understands a chain of command or a problematic pet trying to dominate you and others in the pack and be the ruler!

Is that the definition of friendship? In my book, it isn't!

With time, a friendship bond will form, and only under those conditions will the dog look up to you and be unconditionally faithful.

Can you grasp the message here? You don't need to make friends right away. You just need those around you who will follow.

Eventually, friendships will be forged, and you will have allies for life.

If you are not a leader, you are a follower, and we have both failed! So, take that simple example with you and practice. If you have a dog, practice on him. Or get one. It's a good way to learn how to control tempers and situations.

Another lesson that can apply to the dog example is interpreting body language. Dogs are simple creatures. If they are happy, they wag their tail. Their posture is also one of the indicators. A happy, healthy dog stands up straight with its ears up and its mouth partially open. If it's alert, the mouth closes and the tail stops moving. If its angry, the hair on its back stands up; if scared, one of the tells might be that it pulls its ears back and puts its tail between its legs. They will often lie on their back to demonstrate submission or refuse to offer you their belly up it if they don't want to submit.

WHOLE PACKAGE

You need now worry about the happy dogs, who will readily comply with your requests and follow and accept your dominance.

An angry dog, on the other hand, is another matter. Angry dogs will test you, refuse to give up their Alpha status. Therefore, you need to show them you are game! Stand up straight, look confident (or better, be confident), with your shoulders wide and chest high. Speak sharply and clearly. Make sure they understand what you want from them!

Now, the scared dog is the one to watch for. They will bite if you push them to the limit or run away.

These same rules apply to people. That's how simple and primal we really are. Watch for those signs in people you meet or already know. Learn your friends from your foes. Keep your eye out for those body language hints and signs. Look people in the eye, straight and sharp. Teach yourself to also pay attention to and remember people's names. This is *VERY* important. While making eye contact, learn as much as you can from them. If they look you in the eye at first but eventually look down as they start talking or give you a nod, it means they have realized you are a top dog and are okay with it. They will remain friendly, maybe even too friendly, and will be happy to work with and take instructions from you. That type is not likely to ever challenge you.

Then there are those who will stare long and hard back, challenging and pushing you to your limits! Just remember, it's all a game nature intended us to play and go with it. As long as you know what you are doing, you have the advantage.

There will be times, however, when neither person will look away. This usually escalates into a verbal conflict; here is where your interpretational and academic level and skills will save you. In this phase, as the conflict graduates from visual to verbal, it's crucial to have the confidence to lead the conversation and keep the tempo high and sharp, playing by your rules. This is when those "big" words become your weapon, and you can slay him/her with your intellectual skills. If you pace it right and show an appropriate level of dominance, the opponent will back off and let you assume top-dog position yet again.

Having said this, please don't take the words "conflict," "weapon," "slay," or "fight" too literally.

Most likely, the "conflict" will happen on a mental level, too subtle for most to notice. Most times, you will exchange looks, change postures, and pass a few quiet words back and forth, and the "match" will be over before you know it. Very rarely will it escalate into a physical altercation, and if you've worked on your intellect, education, and vocabulary, that should never be the case.

Nevertheless, you should always be prepared to defend yourself against a threat.

And the third kind you will encounter is the scared animal. Intimidated and fear-filled, it can resort to its lowest means to escape a tight spot. I repeat, these are the most dangerous ones.

Let's look back at the happy "dog" example.

They make a great asset and are proven to follow and obey, as long as you keep them motivated. Same applies to people around you. I'm talking about those working for or under you. Those following you. Help them grow along the way, and you will have a happy pack member moving in harmony with you and all its other members in a great working environment and worry-free time. Praise them often, show them better ways to get the same results, stimulate them financially, and otherwise, but do not make the mistake of becoming too close! Keep your distance, and you will lead forever. If you close that gap between you, everything you worked for will be ruined. The minute they feel equal or better than you, they'll revert to bloodthirsty beasts and challenge your position as leader. They will not just ruin you but also fight among themselves till no one is left. You want to avoid that at all costs, so keep this in mind.

In the second scenario, submitting that Alpha that just wouldn't look down, and by this I mean when you're challenging another strong minded person to follow your lead, you need to be careful how much pressure and for how long you deploy on him/her. If you don't possess the intellectual abilities to make him feel inferior, you might lose that duel. You want to avoid that at all costs as well, so as previously mentioned, prepare ahead of time; assume you will have to use your knowledge and skills at some point, and *PRACTICE*!

Nothing can surprise you if you're ready.

You might find it hard to come out on top sometimes in such encounters, so you also must be prepared to take the conflict to the next level. It's in our nature to fear what we cannot understand or beat.

Only humans, of all nature's creatures, when encountering an opponent stronger and superior to them, will sometimes opt for other ways out. Such as taking their own life before engaging in a fight they know they can't win.

I'm talking about extreme-case scenarios here, which you are unlikely to ever encounter, but I just want to paint the picture for you to help you understand the kind of desperate measures that desperate people may be willing to take in situations from which they perceive no way out.

Keep that in mind. It means that a man, if scared, is extremely unpredictable and ready for anything. And what scares us more than someone we can't stare down or defeat in conversation is someone who's physically superior to us!

So be ready to take that fight to the next, physical level. It's the most primitive way of solving the conflict, but nevertheless, an important one. Now those hours in a gym and/or dojo come into play! It will more likely happen with someone who is less intellectually gifted and, due to their lack of elegance or conversational skills, will reach for this shameful way of demonstrating power. Those are usually easy to tame. Just remember a previous lesson and use only the force necessary for them to realize you can't be beat. Leave them a way out, and 99 percent of the time, they will take it. After that, offer them peace, and you will often gain an accomplice who will never question your authority again.

You will turn them into one of those happy pack members. And you both win!

The scared ones are the hardest to work with, but at the same time, most rewarding when you succeed in changing them. You need to be extra careful and apply the most effort toward this type of human, little by little gaining their trust, showing them you are not a bad guy, that you don't want to hurt or humiliate them. The cautious approach is crucial, and using a mild tone and less offensive posture are a must. Once you let them see you for who you really are, they will recognize your qualities and realize that you desire their presence in the community instead of opposing it. They will then gradually move toward the back of your pack, slowly working their way toward the "Happy" members.

Once you start changing yourself and the people around you, you will realize how rewarding all this is and how much better your life has become!

A leader is the one who knows the way, goes the way and shows the way.

—John C. Maxwell

You will soon realize that New You is attracting a lot of attention. The same sex will gather to get to know and engage in conversation with this shiny and bright personality. Your jokes will be laughed at, and others will follow you in general.

The opposite sex will be charmed by your confidence and intelligence, seduced by your appearance and voice, drawn by your smile and humor, and glued to that Alpha in you because it's the most basic instinct they have. Every female wants to get herself an Alpha male and vice versa. That's been the case since the beginning of time! You will find yourself enjoying the attention sometimes but will become distracted by it on occasion.

I can tell you this from personal experience. And to be

WHOLE PACKAGE

modest and believable, I'll just briefly comment here. A long time ago, I noticed the attention I got everywhere I showed up. It could in part be because I am six feet, four inches tall and usually weigh around 265 pounds.

But I've seen others like me or bigger, and they didn't have nearly the same effect.

I know. You are thinking that this entire Alpha thing had gotten into my head, and I'm seeing things that are not there.

But let me tell you... It's a real thing. Your new attitude and confidence WILL attract attention. Good and bad.

I'm lucky my wife and I have developed full, unconditional trust, or otherwise we would no longer be together.

On the other hand, she gets approached all the time too. And I don't have a problem with that. I understand the concept and trust her completely! That's also part of who I am and my security. And let me tell you, it doesn't matter whether you are tall or short, skinny or overweight. It matters how you carry and present yourself and how confident you are! It shows, and people unconsciously pick up on it! And the good news is, it's something you can work on! So, improve and perfect it! Get all the advantages you can! There are *NO* rules in this game! The sky's the limit! So let loose and explore! You will thank me later!

To sum up the complete package of the Alpha...

Strong posture, head up, shoulders wide, chest high, a sharp, firm look, and a clear, strong voice. Use good language and make solid eye contact when you speak to others. Always look your best and present yourself in the best light. Dress for success! Remember, people are *ALWAYS* judging you, seeking signs of weakness to exploit. Have a ready answer for every possible provocation. If you know you are short or chubby, or are aware of other flaws you might have, practice comebacks from jokes and comments directed to those things! Never make fun of your flaws because to others, it's perceived as a sign of insecurity and discomfort. Usually, we self-deprecate so others don't get that chance!

Avoid doing this at all costs. It just masks your insecurity, and people will see right through it.

Rather, have a good, sharp and witty comeback ready to address any remarks others might make toward you! That way, you will show that you are aware of those flaws but proud of who you are, which is far superior to the person they are or will ever be. Usually, when you shut a few of those up in a hurry, others will not dare challenge you! Also, they will pay you more respect to you afterward, so it's really a win-win situation.

Try to lead the conversation in a room, or if not, listen carefully and discuss the topic thoroughly. *NEVER* get yourself into an argument on topics you are not strong in, but rather, let others discuss them and soak in their knowledge so you can bring up a few points next time. Also, never argue with an expert on a subject. You are not only setting yourself up for failure but will also appear extremely annoying to any others involved. Always think before you act, and try to predict a few possible outcomes.

CHAPTER 14

THERE ARE OTHERS...

There's a double meaning in that title. And I will discuss both.

Those Like You

There are others like you (or like what you're striving to become).

Do not think of those, who are like you, as enemies. They will be that *ONLY* if you make them so. Otherwise, Alphas can co-exist in this society and even complement each other in many ways. If there's another one in your company interested in getting ahead, fast and furious, it doesn't mean that he/she poses a threat! Rather, look at it as healthy competition. What would happen to that Alpha in nature, the leader of a wolf pack, if no one ever challenged him? He would most likely become slow, fat, and overconfident, eventually allowing even a slightly stronger Omega to knock him off that throne!

But nature won't allow that! It ensures that new and younger Alphas will always rise to challenge the top dog and his abilities. Only when he is truly weaker and slower will a new, younger, furious male assume his position, but again, not without a fight! Plus, in that company, there's always room for more than one hungry young Alpha. That's also nature's way of making sure that only the best of the best comes out on top! Same with your social life. Let's say another guy is trying to get a girl you've had your eye on for some time. He will bring out the best in you. Soon you will discover you are capable of things you never dreamed of! Even if she likes you only, she will play along and help in that challenge, help you fight for her attention and eventually, the ultimate prize. We need that kind of challenge in every aspect of our lives to stimulate our senses and test our abilities. Such challenges are equal to military drills, designed to keep you alert and on top of your game!

By repeating such exercises, we learn to act instinctively and fast! We learn to trust our judgment and abilities as opposed to spending precious time in emergency situations calculating odds and options.

Knowledge is a treasure, but practice is the key to it.

—Lao Tzu

Never back down from a challenge. They're good for you. If you have a problem with being challenged and demonstrating your skills, you are most likely insecure about some of them and need to re-evaluate and perfect certain aspects of your game! But if look forward to a challenge and enjoy undertaking one, you are most likely on the track toward greatness! Just keep going, use everything you learn here, and most importantly, apply the skills you've honed and what you've learned about yourself to your advantage. You don't need to know your opponent; you just need to know and trust yourself! And you will never lose!

So instead of staring that work colleague down for

THERE ARE OTHERS...

being ambitious and arguing with your soon-to-be girlfriend about how she responded to that tall, handsome guy flirting with her earlier that day, try to accept all that as a game and play along! You are allowed to play little games too! Do something to impress your boss and watch that nerd at work turn green with envy, or venture into some light flirting with a hot girl at the bar and make your object of desire realize there are others interested in the prize she is about to lose! Have fun with it. Don't take life too seriously! I know what we are trying to achieve here is very important, and as I've said, by all means, use all the resources and strength necessary to get there, but don't forget to enjoy life and its joys in the process. Look at everything as a learning experience, and try to take something new with you from every situation you get thrown into! Trust me when I say this: The race to the top will seem dull and pointless if you forget to enjoy getting there!

One of the most famous Serbian poets, Desanka Maksimovic, wrote a poem that has stuck with me throughout my life. It's short, sweet, and, I've always thought, very romantic.

But I feel like she wrote about much more than love and desire. In fact, I think her words can be incorporated into many things in life. I've included the poem below. Read it, and you'll see what I'm talking about!

Apprehension
by Desanka Maksimovic

*"No... Don't come any closer! I wish to adore
and love your eyes from afar.
For, happiness is real only while you dream of it–
when its illusion tickles our heart.
No... Don't come any closer! There is more magic
in waiting with sweet apprehension and fear.
Just while seeking them out, things appear pure;
It's better to have them just beyond the reach...
No... Don't come any closer! Why would you, and what for?*

Only from great distance stars shine so bright;
Only from afar can we admire it all.
No... Keep your eyes in the distance for me."

My interpretation is that she is talking about love, but can't we apply the same principles to everything?

I believe, and perhaps you agree, that we need to enjoy the journey and not rush to get there. That once we reach our goal, the magic of the process will disappear. I believe that if we don't keep setting routine goals for ourselves, we will fall into the trap of reaching them and then get stuck in the moment, not knowing what to do next!

The greatest danger for most of us is not that our aim is too high and we miss it, but that it is too low and we reach it.

—Michelangelo Buonarroti

My advice to you is to constantly set new, small goals to keep you motivated! Keep the journey alive; keep moving. Keep that carrot in front of the donkey, and it will never run out of steam!

There's so much in life that can motivate us. The world holds endless potential reasons for us to keep growing and bettering ourselves! Learn to motivate yourself and keep going! Train to go the distance, to push your limits. Learn to deal with pain and exhaustion. Visualize the prize and you reaching it! Live that moment in your mind before it happens! Learn to want things to happen, to wish upon it! Wishful thinking is VERY, very important to this process and a skill you must master.

Again, do not make one goal the center of your universe because you will miss out on everything else, and then that prize, once reached, will have little to no meaning! I'll stress this again and will never get tired of repeating it!

THERE ARE OTHERS...

The most important thing in life is *BALANCE!* Find a magic formula to balance your life, and you will hold the universe in your hand! To have such balance in life, you must first find balance within your inner self! Once you have that figured out, the rest should just come along.

A man with outward courage dares to die; a man with inner courage dares to live.

—Lao Tzu

In regards to the above quote, I strongly believe you need both to find your balance!

This brings us to that other group of people we'll now discuss.

Others Not Like You

Finding balance means coexisting with those people too. No wonder, since they make up the majority of the world's population. Don't treat them as your inferiors but as you wish to be treated. Doing good triggers good in return. The same goes for evil! So, before you act, think and *RETHINK*.

Learn not to intimidate such people. Or at least not to the point that it triggers discomfort or fear on their side! Act firm but smile as you do. Look them in the eyes, but let them know you do not plan to get invasive. They will instinctively move out of your way most of the time, but should you bump into one here and there, avoid exerting your strength and dominance to make an example of him/her. Do not feed your ego by torturing the weak and helpless. There's no satisfaction in defeating someone who you already know is not your match. There's no honor in that. Feel compassion instead! Help them if you can. Show them the way. Make them feel worthy. Remember that we all have it in us! Some just don't know it. Remember how you were before you started reading this book. Remember your life. Kind words go a long way. You will find most of these types—those who are not like you—working for or under you in some way. Pay attention and learn proper leadership skills! Take special note of chapter 5, regarding your development, since one goal we are setting here is to be a leader in one way or another. Whether it be a company you run or work at, group of friends you hang out with, a class you are teaching, or a political party that elected you. There are many forms of leadership, and after mastering the lessons in this book, you should be able to fall into the role of leader naturally.

Always remember these words for they describe in essence the art of leadership!

"To lead people, walk beside them.
As for the best leaders, the people do not notice their existence.
The next best, the people honour and praise.
The next, the people fear; and the next, the people hate.
When the best leader's work is done the people say, We did it ourselves!

—Lao Tzu

Let's look carefully at part of Tzu's quote, which I believe is important to highlight.

"As for the best leaders, the people do not notice their existence." This might sound a little confusing to some, so I will clear it up. In another version of this quote, Tzu supposedly said: "A leader is best when people barely know he exists." Tzu is also quoted as saying, "If you want to lead them you must place yourself behind them."

Let's look at the core message I believe Tzu is trying to convey:

THERE ARE OTHERS...

Tzu is implying that people must know who their leader is and follow him, but in doing so, they must also feel like equals and not grow intimidated. That leader must show that he is at the same level as his followers, working as they do and ensuring everyone is made to feel equal and important. To lead by example.

By making those around you happy and motivated, you'll feel the same way. Good vibrations spread like waves, and it's easy to get caught up in the momentum! On a contrasting note, bad vibes can spread even faster and broader; you must keep those at bay! Maintain a positive environment and attitude and do little things that motivate people. Those steps alone will take you a *LONG* way!

Show dignity and respect; don't throw your superiority into other people's faces. No need to point out that you are an Alpha and therefore more worthy than them. You know who does that? Those who feed off the fear of others and must always induce more of it to fix their broken ego. You know the term for this human type, of course.

The Imaginary Alpha.

They constantly herald their best qualities while simultaneously pointing out other people's flaws, publicly displaying them, exposing their weaknesses to cover up for their own failings and insecurities! They are much worse than those they make fun of and torture. And deep down, they know it.

If a person seems wicked, do not cast him away.
Awaken him with your words, elevate him with your
deeds, repay his injury with your kindness. Do not
cast him away; cast away his wickedness.

—Lao Tzu

If you happen across someone like this, try to reason

with them. Use the techniques described in this book to assert your will and help them realize they are wrong and need help. Show them how a true Alpha acts. Show respect after you defeat them! They will most likely refuse to see the truth, but you can always try if you have the time and energy to spare.

I just hope that, by some fortunate twist of fate, they will get their hands on this book, and by an even bigger chance, read it. It might help them recognize themselves and actually take steps toward becoming the very thing they are trying to fake! I wish them luck and hope they see the path and can follow it. Just remember, you must empty the glass before you fill it again.

I sincerely hope I've helped teach you how to live in harmony with those around you. I *KNOW* that by this point in the book, you've learned to live in harmony with yourself.

Next, we'll look at how a specific method of thinking can help you on your journey.

CHAPTER 15

WISHFUL THINKING

Let's discuss this *VERY* important part of your journey. Many books have been written about wishful thinking, a topic that doesn't need much explanation.

I will start by saying wishful thinking can take *POSITIVE* and *NEGATIVE* forms.

Try to think back. Remember times in your life when you wished for something to happen, a certain scenario to play out, and it ended up being so. The day was saved! You know what I'm talking about, a time when you weren't ready for that math test, and the teacher didn't show up to work that day, or you got all the right questions. That time you needed money desperately, and by some stroke of luck, you got a hefty tax return or refund or found a $50 bill in a winter jacket in your closet. When you were thinking about a person you hadn't seen in years and then, bam, the very next day, you ran into them! I know this has happened to you in some way or another, and while there's no scientific proof of any connection between your thoughts and actual events, I like to think it's more than just coincidence or chance when it happens.

To all of us.

I know there are forces at work in this world beyond our understanding and knowledge. I strongly believe that the human mind is capable of unimaginable things! History has born witness to so many miracle-like events! So many great people have left their mark, saying or doing something that became a lasting testament to the power of a strong will and mind! From the beginning of time, empires have been built and then destroyed by greater empires. Wars for dominance and ultimate power have scorched our earth in the past, and many are still burning in the present. It's in our nature to impose power over those inferior and submissive to us.

But what about those little people, the ones who enacted great rebellions? What about those who proved to us that wishful thinking can change one's life?

We see medical miracles every day. People beating cancer after all hope faded. Willing themselves out of illness, never giving up or losing hope! Or those paralyzed who doctors said would never walk again, only to do so against all odds. Look up Nick Vujicic, a man born with no limbs. He went on to become an international motivational speaker for people across the globe, traveling and teaching! Nick lives his life to the best of his ability while telling others to never lose hope! During his talks, he'll often say while lying flat on his belly… "If I fall a thousand times, do you think I'm ever going to give up? NO! I'm going to keep trying and trying until I get up!"

And then he gets up!

And people cry. And laugh. And are overwhelmed with emotions.

I watched one of his talks, and listening to him and seeing him rise had such a powerful impact on me! Standing there with no arms or legs but so powerful and proud in that moment!

I found myself thinking…

If people like him can be positive and work on and improve themselves and their lives, what are the rest of us complaining about?

WISHFUL THINKING

How about that woman and mom, *Angela Cavallo,* who lifted and held a '64 Chevy Impala, which weighed about 3,500 pounds, to prevent her son, whose head got stuck between a wheel and the fender of a car, from choking! She did it just long enough to be helped by nearby neighbours who rushed to their aid.

How many stories have we heard of athletes with superb physical abilities getting beaten by someone less fortunate but who dedicated their life to bettering themselves in that particular sport? I claim that we can beat our genetic code! We can't erase it, but we can become the BEST using what has been given to us! We must learn not only to play to our strengths but also to recognize our weaknesses and work on them. If we constantly avoid what we are not comfortable with, we set ourselves up for failure. Throw yourself out there, face your fears, and do things you are not so good at so you can become better! Practice. Never slack!

There are so many other examples I can list. People who have lost massive amounts of weight, for example! Shows such as *The Biggest Loser, X-Weighted*, and *Heavy* are popular for a reason. If you had watched any of those shows, did you notice improvements in the contestants other than physical? The kind of attitude overall that those who made tremendous progress showed? This is particularly apparent when comparing these winners after the fact to how they appeared in the before footage: lifeless and having given up on life, health, and everything else that is beautiful and worth living and changing for.

And then they start their transformation, and *BAM*!

They take control of their life, and they get angry! Angry at themselves! And they go to work! *YES, WORK!* A hard, long process, but they do it. Look at their eyes; they are clear and determined! They are focused! Hungry for a slice of success pie! Every step takes them closer to that new person they want to become, and they can't wait to get there. Step by step, buckets of sweat and blood and hundreds of healthy, tasteless meals later, they stand proud and new!

They made it!

This holds true with any addiction as well. Drugs, alcohol, etc.

The formula is the same. You just have to follow it, to find it within yourself to do it. Reach deep inside, grab ahold of your inner strength, and apply it to everything you want to achieve!

Wishful thinking is explained very thoroughly in one of my favorite books called *The Secret*, which basically tells us that what we send out to the universe comes back to us.

Meaning that, if you think positively, visualize your goals, and believe you can achieve it, you send positive vibes "out there." And in doing so repeatedly, day after day, eventually, it will come back to you and come true. Now, I don't know whether it's the universe rewarding you or maybe a metaphor for self-confidence and belief in oneself and one's possibilities, but it works.

The same, however, holds true for all the negativity people surround themselves with all the time. Doubts. Fear. Insecurities.

Be very careful about what kind of vibes you're sending out there. You might be setting yourself up for failure. Or success! It's up to you entirely.

Let me go back and explain negative wishful thinking a bit here.

This is where you can sabotage your success. At this point in your journey, I sincerely hope there's no need to be alert about this, for I hope that the previous lessons in this book have helped your attitude become *OPTIMISTIC* and *POSITIVE*.

But it needs to be addressed here just in case. Just as you can help yourself by thinking positively and visualizing goal achievement, you can easily ruin everything and prevent yourself from succeeding by enforcing a negative attitude and negative thinking. I have a friend, who I will not name, but this person has the capability of making himself physically ill by thinking about getting sick and visualizing it. On more

WISHFUL THINKING

than one occasion, I've witnessed him go from perfect health to having a fever, breathing problems, and worse. Just by believing he was getting sick, he was able to change his physical condition and become sick in reality. This is not a joke. The condition, called **hypochondria**, is very real. This disorder consists of the fear of having a serious condition. I believe, in the case of my friend, his fear is strong enough for him to actually live the symptoms and become ill.

So, HAPPY THOUGHTS all the way, and don't fear failure!

There's another kind of negative wishful thinking, and this one is out of your hands. It's such thinking from those around you.

There is one way you can manage this issue to a certain degree, and that's by selectively choosing those you surround yourself with. But you will still encounter many negative wishful thinkers who, on a daily basis, will feed you negativity and doubt.

Your defense against those will come in the form of everything you've learned here so far, namely, your confidence, self-esteem, and knowledge of yourself and the world around you.

My advice is to do a very thorough, hard assessment of yourself and your capabilities, become aware of your abilities and worth, and never doubt it again.

That will be all you'll ever need against naysayers.

Have you heard the story about the difference between cows and buffalos?

In the event of a great storm, a herd of cows will try to outrun it by running away from it.

In doing so, eventually, the storm will catch up with them, and not only will it blow at full impact all over them but for a prolonged period as well since they're still running, thus prolonging their time spent inside the storm.

On the other hand, buffalos will run at full force, head-on toward the storm. Since they run through the storm at full throttle, they manage to get out of it sooner, thus spending much less time enduring the effects of it.

That story fascinates me on so many levels. So primal and simple yet a very useful teaching tool for those like me, trying to teach people to face their fears and problems head-on instead of running away from them, hiding and procrastinating.

There will be times when we are going to slip. Some events in our life will hit us hard and we will get sidetracked. It happens to all of us. It happened to me too. I gained a massive amount of weight at one point! I'm talking about two hundred pounds overweight if not more—an extremely high amount for me since I've always kept careful control over my training and eating and have preserved a healthy body and body image. Life got in the way: personal problems, a job that took me away from healthy choices, etc.

But no one and nothing was to blame but me! One day I took a deep breath, remembered who I was and what I was capable of, and took back charge of my life and set out on a weight loss journey. You have to remember I was not just overweight but extremely out of shape. I had high blood pressure that was threatening my health. I couldn't run; even walking was somewhat of a task at that point. So, I started my comeback and never looked back! Little by little, my cardio condition improved, and my muscle strength and volume came back slowly. Day after day, I trained and followed a healthy diet plan till I reached my goal. One short year later, I was a hundred pounds lighter and in the best shape of my life! I never had any doubts that I could do it! I never stopped to think! I just kept pushing and pushing, and I got to my destination, making it happen in a relatively short time, too! Many others have shared similar experiences, and I know there are people out there getting excited about taking those first baby steps toward their weight loss or muscle-building goal or tackling whatever it is that is holding you back!

I know it's a cliché and has been said millions of times, but it truly doesn't matter how hard or how many times you fall, as long as you can get up and continue! You must know yourself! Dig deep inside your soul and find your very bottom because only then can you realize your very top!

Another example is that of academic achievement. Look at the good lawyers, doctors, and scientists out there.

Do you think any of them came from a rich family where they had everything on a silver plate, fed to them with a golden spoon? Those are usually failures in school, and for a simple reason! They are fulfilling someone else's dreams! I will take a moment here to request one little thing from you! And it's *EXTREMELY* important!

Don't ruin lives of your children by making them follow your own unfulfilled dreams or paths you lacked the courage or determination to follow.

Let them find their own road to greatness and, more importantly, happiness, and just be there as a support and their biggest cheerleader. Offer advice, but don't force it onto them. And enjoy watching them with a sense of pride as they prosper.

It's as simple as that. So many parents do this despite the consequences such a path has on their children. Your children can never achieve your dreams; they must follow their own!

It will be easier on them if they have your full support, but best help would be to stand by their side and watch them grow and become what they want to be! Most successful business people, in fact, come from poor families. They know all too well how it is to **NOT** have. They grew up that way, and they've had enough! The Alpha inside them awoke and roared at the idea of enduring that kind of life with anger and might! They don't want that for themselves or their children! And they will do anything necessary to break that cycle! Work through college, do extra activities at school, study extra hard, and never stop until they succeed! Because nothing is as hard for them as going back to the life they hated! That's why they became successful, because they were hungry and motivated, knew full well where they didn't want to end up, and kept pushing forward, further and further away from the gutter they came from. Aren't they a perfect example of wishful thinking? All they want is to not be who they were at the beginning. Isn't that what we want for us here? To get as far away from that Omega we once were and never look back? Keep moving forward and crushing obstacles in your path! You need to be that winner in your mind first, to visualize yourself at the final destination and then follow the yellow brick road until you get there physically!

CHAPTER 16

THE PEOPLE YOU LOVE AND WHO LOVE YOU

As you move forward in your journey, the people in your life will start noticing changes in your behavior and personality. It will become obvious that something is going on with you.

I strongly suggest that you sit down and have a talk with your spouse, children, and/or others you are extremely close with and explain what will be happening from that day on. There are many reasons for that. I will name just a few below.

Your spouse is your best friend and will be in your corner throughout this journey! You want to get her/him on board. The ideal scenario would be if you both set off on a journey together, supporting each other, pointing out each other's potential mistakes, and so on along the way—a perfect scenario for you both! So, when you explain to them your goals, try to instill enthusiasm in them as well. See if you can get them excited to join you, and stress how much it would mean to you if they would also take part! Some will agree, but others won't. That is okay. Just make sure that they understand what is going on and ask them to be supportive and have patience with New You while you're in training.

Remind them often how important their love and support is to you and that you aren't doing this just for yourself but for everybody else in your little community as well! I guarantee they will eventually comply and might just be open to some of the steps involved. By all means, let them join! Take them to the gym! Or let them sign up for your class on learning Japanese or enroll them as your partner in a salsa class! You will see that they will, little by little, break out of their shell and become more interested in the whole Alpha process! It's only natural to follow your partner's growth, and it will come to them! As you become more educated, they will work to follow in your stead. The better shape you get into, the more they'll want to work on their appearance! The more powerful you both become, the stronger the bond will be that's holding you together. The greater your personal growth, the more levels you will base your relationship on! Let yourself be free! Do everything with passion! Enjoy every moment of this glorious transformation!

I guarantee that your sex life will explode. More confidence brings more pleasure! Feeling good about yourself will let you enjoy your time in the bedroom to the fullest. Being capable of doing more in life will teach you to explore your sexuality, and your passion meter will skyrocket! That's yet another reason why it's so important to let your loved ones in on this little secret we all share here! Otherwise, your newfound creativity and stamina in bed, social confidence, newfound charm, and new attention you're getting might lead them to suspect you're having an affair or something similar. And can you blame them?

All of a sudden, people will witness a different you. It can't be hidden, and why hide it anyway? Display it proudly; use it for motivation for future steps. As you progress, and hopefully your partner does too, incorporate more people by telling them you're on a journey! Make them realize you are not to be taken for granted anymore! Perform little

THE PEOPLE YOU LOVE AND WHO LOVE YOU

demonstrations of your progress to keep them on their toes! Have as much fun with all this as you like!

It's your life and decision; do what you may with it!

Another reason to share this with all the people in your inner circle: You need *ALL* the help you can get to stay on the right path! You'll need love and support from your friends and family! And in most cases, they will be supportive, especially after they start noticing improvements and a new level of self-awareness and motivation in you! Don't keep this secret to yourself! Let others educate themselves on this subject! Let them borrow this book and read it! Then discuss it among your group and compare ideas, analyze their meanings, and maybe set some goals together! Healthy competition is always the best motivation, so try to work in conjunction, and all sides will benefit! Show them how much fun they can be, how much stronger they can become for themselves and the people they love! You will notice that slowly but surely, your enthusiasm and optimism will catch on! Good is contagious, and little by little, you will help them better their lives. You will feel energized every time you light up the room, complete one little task, and feel how the people you care about support you. Now they're your team, your cheerleaders, and they want to see you succeed as much as they want success for themselves!

You will need them at times when things are not going so great. When you feel doubt and fear creep in and start to question your motives and goals. It will help you overcome self-doubt and keep you focused on the prize!

And don't forget to give as much as you take! Be there for those who are there for you. If they trip and fall, help them up. In doing so, you will also be helping yourself.

My family and friends have played such a *HUMONGOUS* role in my life, starting with my parents early on who taught me core values, good manners, common sense, self-love, and many of the other things I've talked about. This played a crucial role in shaping me into the person I am today. I learned about respect and hard work from my grandparents.

I witnessed my grandma struggle and my mom toil and succeed as a single parent with two young children. I learned about courage, strength, and persistence from them as well. I learned about love. My other grandpa, my father's father, was a very influential man in a high position. I learned pride, confidence, compassion toward others, leadership skills, and righteousness by following his example.

The teachers at my school planted in me a strong sense of respect toward authority and intellectual superiority.

In the army, I learned all about hierarchy, teamwork, respect toward my superiors, and following orders. And to strive toward a position in life in which I wouldn't need to follow the orders of others, but rather have mine followed by those under me.

In the course of one's life, you take little bits and pieces of everyone you come into contact with! Always remember that *EVERY* person you meet has *SOMETHING* to teach you. Pick out that knowledge and take it with you on your quest. You can learn even from the unlikeliest source! Always keep that in mind and keep your mind open! Often, in life, you will learn something subconsciously and realize it only when the situation calls for such a solution. Then you will remember the person who taught you that solution and realize what a valuable lesson it was! Never underestimate the power of learning! Your mind and body do it twenty-four-seven. It never rests. We also learn from our dreams things we subconsciously want and desire. Sometimes in a dream, you might realize someone means more to you than your conscious mind is letting on. Or we'll see solutions to problems that have kept us from growing for a long time. In a dream, your mind is telling you things. Learn to listen. Take your time and have patience.

The best things in life are the people we love and care about! I love my people and would do anything for them as I know they would for me!

THE PEOPLE YOU LOVE AND WHO LOVE YOU

Success unshared is total failure.
—John Paul DeJoria

Another thing I want to request, and this desire was inspired by events in which a few people who were dear to me passed away before their time, is to NEVER wait too long to tell others what lies in your heart because it will eventually become too late, and there will be nothing you can do once they cross over from this world onto their next journey, whatever that might be.

Never fail to let a person know what they mean to you! *Show* gratitude and love. Don't put it off. Make sure you tell people how much you love them and what they are to you in this life!

The bitterest tears shed over graves are for words left unsaid and deeds left undone.
—Harriet Beecher Stowe

CHAPTER 17

WRAPPING IT ALL UP INTO THE COMPLETE NEW YOU!

I am *REALLY* proud of you for finishing this book. Even if you decide not to follow through, you will still take a great deal from the book with you and apply it consciously or unconsciously throughout your future life. But if you truly love yourself and the people around you, how can you not wish to change? Why willingly keep yourself a slave, basically, of your limitations? How can you choose The Matrix over freedom, blue skies, and a life of laughter and enjoyment? I can't answer that question.... Only you can. But will you? Look in the mirror and talk to that inner you. Try to reason with it. Take a good look first! Is that really your reflection? Is that who you are? Or is it the voice taking human form, doing what it is supposed to, fulfilling its duties?! You must recognize your enemy if you ever dream of defeating it! And remember, it can look like a friend, innocent and pure, but **will** hold you back all your life! Dragging you down as you fight to swim and stay afloat! I can't teach you everything, and that is the beauty of it all!

OMEGA TO ALPHA

I ask you to *NEVER* use what you've learned here to hurt someone, be it financially, socially, or physically! Creating monsters with this book was not my intention, and if I did, as much as it is your failure as a student, I share the blame as the teacher. So, if you find yourself pursuing this journey for the wrong reasons, please stop! Once that monster is unleashed, it will hurt many, including yourself! And it will reflect how much you misunderstood me and the book. That is a sure path to failure in the eyes of others, you and I included! Instead, better yourself for a noble cause! Make this work as much for others as it does for you! Never forget to care for another being, to share and teach! Do not rush to get too powerful too fast. That will add to the risk of losing sight of the real cause you embarked upon this quest for in the first place.

I know that different people will have different motives! Some of you want money, others want power, and still others want attention from the opposite sex. Some are just tired of being who they are and want to make a change! Whatever the personal reason is that made you take that first step in a million-mile journey, make sure it's the right one. Start with the wrong cause from the beginning, and you are destined for doom. So, before you even think about changing, learn why you want to in the first place. Find a good reason. And set a good first goal. I believe that all of you, good or bad, at the end of this journey, will be completely different people.

You will *TRULY* learn who you are by putting yourselves through tests many times over. You will be able to shed all the bad you ever had lingering deep inside of your soul, and find that through good, you become truly enlightened!

So, as all things come to an end, allow me to wrap this up in a few essential things that I feel are most important for everyone to learn on a course of this journey.

These don't come in particular order, but are essentially very important to remember and live by.

Respect

Respect everyone, friend or foe. In doing so, you will make sure not to turn friends into enemies and are far more likely to turn your enemies into friends eventually. Respect draws respect! Even the most seasoned fighter respects the opponent who respects them back!

Love

Show love and give praise! Never shy away from letting others know you love them! A friend, brother, parent, spouse... It doesn't matter! Showing and feeling love unlocks hidden chambers of your soul and will make you a better person! Love is a powerful weapon! Find and treasure it, and it will fuel your life energy forever!

Chivalry

Set a code of honor and follow it daily! Better yourself and others! Show people right from wrong. Help them solve conflicts in a constructive way! Be the one to absorb the necessary impact to teach others the greater good! Don't be afraid to stand for those who can't stand for themselves against injustice!

Courage

Be courageous. Never back down! Show no fear and learn how to control it! It's okay to be afraid at times. We are only human. Learning how to contain and prevent it from becoming our worst enemy is a challenge! Fear can be your ally or your doom! It can numb your senses, cloud your judgment, and slow your reactions! Understand fear and conquer it! Putting yourself in situations that require you to control your fear will strengthen your instincts and speed up your reaction time!

Loyalty

Stay true to those who are true to you. Never play them wrong or change sides when doing so might suit you better! Choose your team and stick to it, absorbing negative impacts as much as you absorb success when times are good. Show them you care. Put them before you sometimes! No team wins every time, no matter how good they are. What they can always do, however, is stick together, no matter the outcome! Everybody can hold together during happy times! True tests of loyalty come when times get tough! Be sure to stay true to those you love and care for, through the good and bad alike.

Practice

Repeat routines over and over! Practice makes perfect! Apply this rule to everything you do. Do not underestimate the importance of this part of the process! It can make or break you when the opportunity presents itself!

Sense of Self

Never mistake *MACHOISM* for being an *ALPHA* as they are two very different things. In fact, they are about as far apart on the spectrum as they can get. Acting macho, or tough and untouchable, is not an attitude we should want for ourselves and is certainly not what others desire to see from you! People who act macho are, in general, insecure and troubled by issues they have dealt with since childhood. Those were the school bullies, the ones who always picked fights in the bar (but always against an opponent inferior in some way, never an equal or stronger). They come in the form of ambitious business people who walk over others to close the deal! Sometimes these are faces of the law, so tortured by feelings of failure and low self-worth that they reach for any source of power available to make them feel better about themselves! Such people, instead of using their badge and gun to defend and protect, exploit their power in a desperate attempt to feel superior. We've all encountered this type at some level! Police officers, customs officers, and government representatives who take great satisfaction in wielding control over your life in some way! We talked about them before—the Fake Alphas! They hold positions within our system that give them perfect opportunities to enforce their wills and ways on others!

This is not the kind of person you ever want to become. So, you need to ensure you possess the positive, confident sense of self needed to help you draw the line at the beginning, the one you'll never cross. That way, you won't become—as mentioned previously in the book—a monster to everyone, including yourself!

Honesty

Be honest and righteous in everything you do! I believe that honesty is recognized by others and will prompt honesty from them as well!

Be a straight shooter! Speak and demand the truth! Teach your kids not to lie! Not even small, white lies! Remember that constantly choosing the lesser of two evils is still choosing evil!

Honor

This one sums up all the previous ones. In that one word, so much meaning is summoned! Honor is a higher state and must be mastered! And it must be earned by fulfilling the previous tasks and exercises mentioned in this book. Honor is easy to lose if you are not careful and, once lost, much harder to regain! Remember that and be careful! Even if honor is all you have in life, you can still die happy and with a sense of accomplishment!

Intelligence

Wisdom is key in training yourself on which battles to choose! To best grasp your strengths and act accordingly! Understanding your opponent will go far in understanding their motives and will help prevent you from underestimating them, no matter who he/she may be. It's too late to be sorry once a battle is lost. Use your brain to plan ahead. Follow the plan. Have a backup plan or two. Develop strategies for any action and perfect it. Spend time and effort before execution! Remember, if you take care of the little things, the big stuff will fall in place.

Everyone's journey will be different! Along the way, you will get to write your own book and call it life! Mark your experiences, the obstacles you faced, the methods you used, and how many attempts it took! You will need that journal when you find someone to pass your knowledge on to! The more you remember from your quest, the better equipped your student will be! Remember, though it's easy to follow in the footsteps of others, in doing so, you lose *YOUR* way! It's better to make footsteps in the fresh snow, walk your way, and arrive on your own!

When you look back on your journey, you will see many inspired to follow in your footsteps and even more leaving their prints in the snow field we call life! Either way, you should be proud of your positive influence, and never forget to keep walking! Our journey never really ends.

Once again, as everything in this world falls under nature's laws, our time is limited, and the end of the road is inevitable. No matter how much we wish it weren't so, no matter how our mind wants to endure, we need to make peace with nature and its rules and accept that nothing is forever, that all things, big and small, eventually come to an end. Mother Nature alone endures to see the beginning and end of all things. You need to reconcile that fact long before your number is up. Just as I taught you, plan ahead to avoid surprises along the way. For your own good and the well-being of those around you.

WRAPPING IT ALL UP INTO THE COMPLETE NEW YOU!

Once you are ready for your next journey—the one beyond this world—you must be just as ready bid goodbye to all those who meant something to you, give last instructions, spend time with loved ones, and prepare to go where others can't follow. If at that last moment of inner peace, when you reflect on your life, you can honestly say that you have no regrets, your purpose on this earth was fulfilled. You can kiss your beloveds goodbye and be sure they will find their way. That all the guidance from you they'll ever need is already carried in their hearts and minds. You will know you taught them well and made them as strong as possible, enabling them to continue your legacy long after you are gone. At that moment, you will feel proud and happy, and nothing in this life will matter more. Inner peace will make your parting easier. Remember, it doesn't matter how much time you spent among them; what matters is how many lives and hearts you touched and good memories you created! And that is what a real Alpha does. It recognizes its time and the right moment to pass the torch. In doing so, you also know you have created other Alphas who will carry it just as well, if not better, for generations to come.

Ask yourself at that moment of truth: "What will I be remembered by?"

If we did everything right, the answer will be there, in our hearts! And I wish you that from the bottom of my heart, just as I do for myself!

CHAPTER 18

AUTHOR'S NOTE

Take care with the end as you do with the beginning.

—Lao Tzu

When I told people I was writing a book, at first, some of them thought I was joking. Then I was faced with some negative inputs.

"You'll never finish it."

"You'll never publish it!"

Such statements came from people I don't really know well and who apparently don't know me at all! To all those doubters and naysayers, I would like to say, please read my book for your sake. I'll even give you a free copy if you can't afford it, but stop being who you are now, or your whole life will be wasted. You'll be sorry at the end over your old ways, but by then, it will be too late. Some things, you'll discover then, you can't change or better! Those kinds of folk, the ones who fail to believe in you, who tell you what you can't do, are who I've been warning you about! Pay no attention to their words! They will sabotage everything you set out to do if given half the chance. Try to help them after you've finished your journey, but do not listen to their negativity! Even the greatest nonsense, if spoken a million times to you, will start to make sense eventually!

To those others, the majority of people who know me well, thank you for the support you've given me. Most of this book was inspired by you all. I'm grateful that you are in my life and I can call you my friends.

My *TEAM*!

I dedicate this book to all those who stood and still stand by my side and root for me! They know I can! I've proved it many times over in my life! You are the ones I want to share everything good in my life with! And I know I don't have to ask you to help me absorb the bad. You always do!

In the end, I would like to mention and express thanks and love to a few very special people who contribute to my strength and dedication to do better EVERY SINGLE DAY.

My team. My foundation. My inspiration. My pride and my joy.

My family, whom I am proud of beyond words. I love you more than you will ever be able to comprehend.

You all believed in me, and stuck by my side through life, no matter what.

I want to thank my Dad, for giving a great example to follow, and for being a great father to me, even if it was just for a brief time.

I want to thank my Mom, for being a wonderful example of kindness, love, courage and sacrifice. For teaching me to love and have faith in myself and others. For believing in me and encouraging me every step of the way.

For passing onto me her amazing gift of literacy and the ability to convey my thoughts into beautiful words.

I hope I make you as proud as I feel, when I think of you all.

There are many of those who I have or had in my life, who inspired me, and I want to thank you all for the contribution and impact you made, sometimes unknowingly, thus changing me personally and my life in general.

AUTHOR'S NOTE

It's said that we are the sum of our experiences, and that includes not just good ones, but unpleasant ones as well. Those uncomfortable moments, if not even more so than pleasant ones, shaped us into who we are today.

Every mistake we took the lesson from, every time someone treated us poorly and caused us pain or discomfort and every time someone disappointed you, affected you in some way. You either grew, adapted or learned from it.

I would like to also thank those who caused me to better myself and grow IN SPITE of what bad things they did to me. Those were awesome motivational and teaching moments for me. I gained power from fighting hardship and grew stronger and bigger in the process.

Even as I finished my manuscript and went through the process of inquiring and learning about book publishing, there were others who wanted to meddle and discourage me and make me quit.

Some have inquired: "So, how big is this book going to be? Did you look up book standards? A novel must be a minimum of sixty thousand words..." That's three hundred pages—well, if you use Word software for your document specs, a certain-sized font, etcetera.

I went online and checked those ridiculous numbers and formulas. How is an author supposed to predetermine how many words or pages will comprise their book? How do you measure what you have to say? Are there people out there who will eschew a book because it is shorter than a longer one at the same price? I don't think so.

Truth is, I'm not in this for money! I want my story heard! I want to inspire others to do the same or better! To offer you my hand to pull yourself out of the gutter, quicksand, or whatever else you feel you're stuck in! I want to be a part of the solution, not the problem!

So, I decided to write as many words as it took for me to say all I needed to. When I put my last thought on paper, taught you everything I felt I needed to, shared every relevant experience I've had, and included every other little detail I felt was important, **that** was when I knew I was done. Whether my last punctuation mark ended after word number twenty thousand or two hundred thousand in the book made no difference to me. Sometimes what needs to be said must take a short, simple form for people to understand.

Having said that, I feel I'm reaching the end of the line. I believe strongly that, at this point, I've said everything I intended to.

I believe I've succeeded in arming you with the weapons and tools necessary for you to figure this out on your own. But before I let you go out into the world, with your eyes now open, I feel obligated to give you this last piece of advice. Because the powers we are unlocking here are serious and not to be taken lightly.

Be righteous. Be compassionate. Stand up for those who can't do so for themselves.

Be honorable and brave. And above all, never, and I repeat, NEVER use your powers to harm others. Your strength is not an excuse to walk over anyone.

I will finish with Jesse Jackson's quote and ask that you take it with you and reflect on it every time you feel superior and strong.

THE ONLY TIME YOU SHOULD LOOK DOWN AT SOMEONE IS WHEN YOU ARE HELPING THEM UP!

Dejan Garalejic is a life coach, author and entrepreneur, with an education and background in Social work. He is utilizing his life and work experience and vast knowledge to help clients in various fields, from nutrition, training and weight loss, business, general self-empowerment, to teaching his protégés about the art of social interaction and success in online dating as well as social networking in general.

Originally born in former Yugoslavia, now Serbia, Dejan had to face hardship from an early age. That culminated in his recruitment by the Serbian Military in 1993, which got him under the rigorous training in the Navy, as part of the elite Scuba diving Special Ops unit, where he mastered combat and survival skills, and attained higher sense of discipline, self-preservation and honor.

In addition to his current work in motivation and coaching, Dejan is the founder and owner of the fitness oriented meal preparation company Deals on Meals, where he combines his knowledge in nutrition and training, education in Culinary Arts and love of food preparation to bring perfectly balanced nutrition closer to his clients.

His contribution doesn't stop there. He's rounding up his current life accomplishment with the newest project from his workshop, a novel that will reveal and explore the more imaginative, and mysterious side of him, as well as having plans to publish his work in Serbian language that consist of poetry and short stories.